Kennedy Holbrook

How?

or, Spare hours made profitable for boys and girls

Kennedy Holbrook

How?
or, Spare hours made profitable for boys and girls

ISBN/EAN: 9783337848774

Printed in Europe, USA, Canada, Australia, Japan

Cover: Foto ©Andreas Hilbeck / pixelio.de

More available books at **www.hansebooks.com**

HOW?

OR

Spare Hours Made Profitable

For Boys & Girls

By Kennedy Holbrook.

Illustrated.

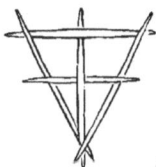

New York:

Worthington Co., 747 Broadway.

1887.

PREFACE.

ALTHOUGH this book is ostensibly a "boy's book," many things which it contains are equally useful to girls ; and have been tried by the latter with entirely satisfactory results. In fact, it was to afford amusement and occupation, on rainy Saturdays and during the long vacation, to the children of both sexes in my own family, that the book was first written ; and it was only an afterthought which led me to give it to the public.

Everything it contains has been deduced from my own experience or that of some trustworthy friend. While it has been my aim to meet the wants of children of all ages and in every condition of life, I have studiously avoided every subject which might be a source of anxiety to the most careful parent.

It is with the hope that this little work may fulfill its mission in other families where it may be received, as happily as it has done in mine, that I send it on its way.

THE AUTHOR.

OCTOBER, 1886.

INDEX.

HOW?

OR,

SPARE HOURS MADE PROFITABLE.

THE WINDMILL PUPPET.

THIS amusing little puppet is very easily constructed, and, like several other mechanical toys in this book, furnishes much entertainment for the little folks. Even the baby will sit in her high chair, half-hours together, watching the little man turning his crank, while she claps her tiny hands and crows at so delightful an exhibition of untiring energy.

Cut from cardboard a disc like Fig. 2, which shall measure about six inches across; then by means of a ruler draw the lines *a b c d;* half-way between these points make four others, corresponding to *e f g h;* and lastly, between all these, still another set of lines. Make the circle, *m*, one-and-a-half inches in diameter, and with a pair of sharp scissors cut through all these lines, to the edge of the smaller ring. Bend one edge of each of these triangular pieces slightly upward, as indicated by the shading, and the opposite edge downward; also bend a piece of wire a foot long, so as to form the crank indicated in the illustration.

Next make a frame-work for the figure to rest upon : this should consist of a three-cornered piece of wood, six inches long for the bottom, a stick six or seven inches long for the upright, and lastly, the support for the upper part of the wire, with a small hole in one end for the latter

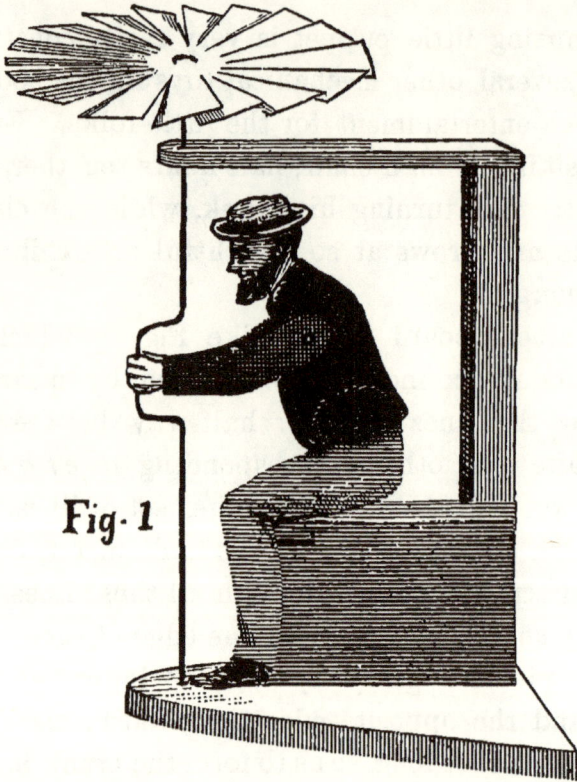

Fig. 1

to pass through.   Fasten these pieces together with small brad-nails, and secure the upright to the bottom piece by a screw or nail passing up from below.   The wire, having the crank already bent in the proper place, may now be passed up through the hole, and the other end sunk down into another, bored a short distance into the bottom board, directly below the upper one. Then the wire may be fastened to the windmill, by passing it through a little one side, then back again through on the other side of the center ; twisting the end once or twice about the main stem beneath the windmill ; it now turns with the windmill, and it is needless to say that the friction in the holes should be as slight as possible.

The figure is to be cut from a piece of cardboard and is made in five pieces. The lower half, which comprises the box, legs, and body up to the dotted line, is in one piece ; the head and body to the lower edge of the belt, consists of two pieces, cut precisely alike, and lapping on either side of the lower part of the body over the dotted line, to give strength to the image. A pin

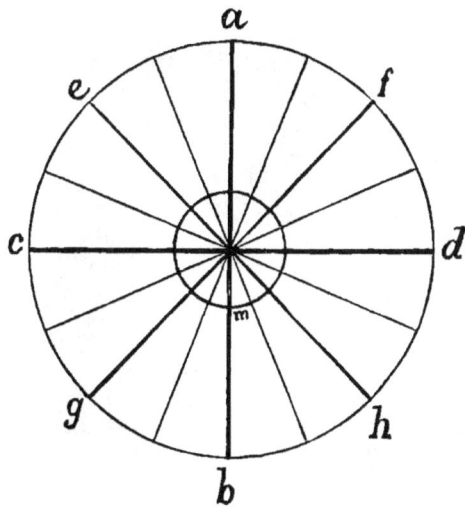

Fig. 2

passed through the belt, and bent down on the other side, will hold it in place, and allow sufficient play to the figure. There are two arms, cut from the same pattern, and pivoted at the shoulders with another pin. The hands are finally brought together, with the crank between them, and lightly secured on either side with two or three stitches.

To impart life to this creation, it is placed over a furnace register through which the hot air is briskly rising. If the machine works easily, the current of air above a stove may suffice.

THE FLYING WHIRLIGIG.

This amusing toy consists of an empty spool with two pins driven into its head, as seen in the figure. With a pair of pliers break off the heads of the pins before driving them in position, then take a piece of soft wood and make a spindle, like that represented in the figure at *A*, and drive another headless pin into the small end. Lastly, cut from a piece of cardboard a figure like the one marked *B*, making three holes, *a a a*, with the point of a darning-needle, corresponding to the two pins in the spool and the one in the spindle.

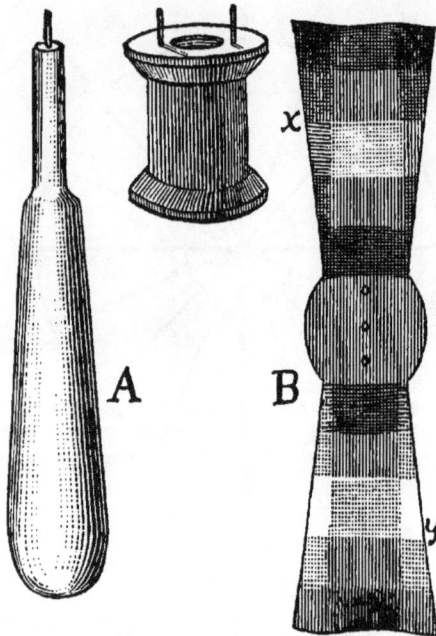

Bend the edges marked *x* and *y* in opposite directions.

Now place the spool on the spindle and wind a piece of twine around the spool; then place the piece of pasteboard upon the top, letting the pins pass up through the row of holes in its center.

Holding the machine upright in the left hand, with a quick movement of the right, jerk the string from the spool, and the cardboard will fly through the air with a very graceful motion.

If stripes of color are added to the ends, as seen in the cut, a much prettier effect is produced while the whirligig is in operation. These stripes can be painted in red, white, and blue water colors, or may be formed by pasting on narrow strips of bright-colored paper.

If the first trial does not succeed, wind the string in the other direction, or put on the "card flyer," with the other side next the spool. The same causes which make it soar away in the one case will hold it yet more firmly to the spool in the other.

HOW TO MAKE A BOOK.

Do any of my boy readers know how to make a book? Not the fine volumes turned out by the thousand in our great publishing houses, but the little individual books made by boys and girls, and needing for their construction only an old used-up ledger, a small tin pan of paste, and scraps cut from newspapers or books. These bits may consist simply of poems, or they may be "a little of all sorts."

I recently saw a very nice book of this kind made by a boy of twelve, which was composed entirely of humorous pictures and jokes, culled from several illustrated and daily papers, one or two almanacs, and various other chance publications, which he had collected during the

year. Whenever he found any bright or witty thing, he
would carefully preserve the clipping by putting it in a
large paper box he kept in a convenient place for that
purpose.

He reserved the pasting for rainy days and winter evenings, and as he took much pains with the arrangement
and neat appearance of his book, this operation was
necessarily slow, and formed a pleasant occupation for
many hours which would otherwise have been wasted.

In making such a book, do not try to complete it in a
week or even a month, but let it, like my boy friend's,
furnish amusement for a year.

Get your father and mother interested, and ask them to
save any scraps they may see, and think appropriate for
the purpose.

A handsomely bound scrap-book, specially designed for
this use, would certainly be the most desirable thing to
have; but if such a book cannot be obtained, an old ledger
does very nicely in its place, and if, after it is completed,
you cover it carefully with a piece of smooth brown paper
and print its title neatly on the back, it will look very
well on any table where you may wish to keep it.

If the latter is used, cut from it every other two leaves,
reserving the third, through the book. Next be careful
to trim all your clippings neatly, leaving no extra paper
beyond the edges. Fit the different slips nicely on the
pages, filling the little spaces left from the longer articles
with any little jokes or bits of poetry you may have.
Frequently a whole piece of newspaper poetry is hardly
worth preserving, but some one of its stanzas may be very

pretty and just the thing to fill up a place you may have left.

It is well to collect all these little things you can find, for they always come in nicely when pasting, and your book looks much better when finished if the original surface is entirely covered.

THE SNAKE.

Cut from a piece of Bristol board, or stiff paper, a circle measuring four inches in diameter ; then with a pencil mark it like Fig. *A.* With your paints and pencil make its head as nearly like a snake's as possible ; and mark the body with stripes or checks, as your fancy may dictate. Cut

A

through the deep black line, put a pin through the dot on the tail, and drive it into a slender stick of wood, which must be held or caught over the stove or register. The rising current of heated air causes the snake to revolve and apparently writhe, in a very natural manner. This little toy, so simple in its con-

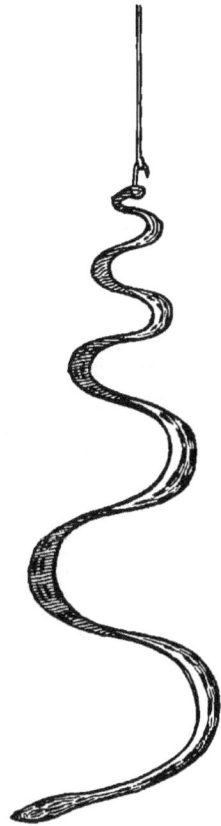

struction, affords an endless amount of entertainment to the little folks of the family, and is well worth the trouble and time you may spend in making it.

The hot air from a lamp or gas jet will also impart activity to this mimic reptile.

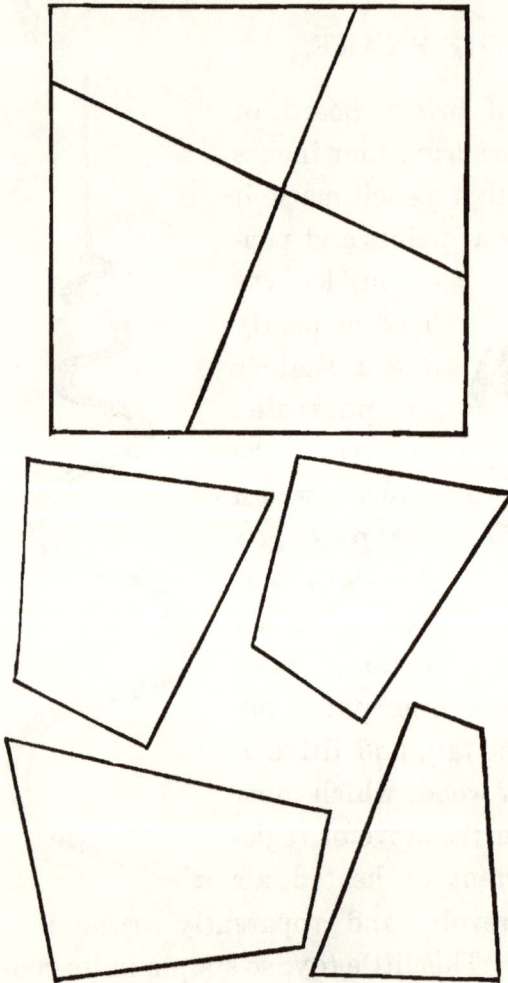

THE DIVIDED SQUARE PUZZLE.

Take a square of paper or cardboard, and cut it into four pieces, as shown in the engraving. Now try to put them back in the form of a square. This seemingly simple puzzle, has kept our young people busy a whole evening, and was only accomplished at last by marking each piece before it was cut apart.

EXPERIMENT WITH TWO PIECES OF GLASS.

Procure two pieces of glass about six inches square, join any two of their sides, and separate the opposite sides with a piece of wax, so that their surfaces may be at a slight angle; immerse this apparatus about an inch in a basin of water, and the water will rise between the plates and form a beautiful geometrical figure called a hyperbola.

THE GRIMACING FACE.

Take a card one-and-one-half inches wide, and fold  around it a piece of unruled note paper, so that the card can easily slide up and down; then paste this case on the under side. Now cut three holes in the paper for the eyes and mouth, as seen in *A*; place the strip of card within this and mark the points for the eyes and root of tongue; then slipping it out once more, the eyes can be carefully finished, and the tongue cut to fit in the mouth, and to extend some distance down on the chin, see Fig. *B*.

Then by putting the two pieces together, pulling the tongue in its place through the opening, very amusing expressions can be produced, by simply moving the pasteboard up and down in the paper. Fig. *C* represents the two parts put together.

A GOOD BALL.

Take a round, well shaped orange; cut it evenly into quarters, numbering them at one end to aid in putting the parts together again. Next cut out of kid four pieces exactly like the four pieces of orange peel; then, with strong linen thread, sew over and over three seams, thus joining the four pieces, but leaving one seam open. In putting together be careful to place 1 next to 2, and so on, just as they were in the orange. Ravel out an old yarn stocking, or cut into narrow strips an old cashmere one, and after making a little round ball of any soft woolen material, commence winding it evenly with the raveled yarn, trying occasionally if it is near the size of the kid covering. When nearly large enough wind it in such a way that it shall just fit the cavity, and then carefully sew up the remaining side.

Great care should be exercised in forming the inner ball, and in cutting the kid. The wrists of old kid gloves make capital coverings. An old rubber overshoe cut in very fine strips and wound carefully, forms a nice center, but it is better to use the soft wool yarn next the cover, as it is more pliable and makes a better shaped ball.

Prepare this ball during your leisure moments in the long winter evenings; and it will then be ready for the first game, when the bright spring sunshine reminds you of summer sports once more.

AMUSING EXPERIMENT WITH TOOTH-PICKS.

Take five tooth-picks, weave them together, as seen in the illustration, which perhaps is easiest done by holding the three diverging ones between the thumb and fore-finger of the left hand at the point *a*, and insert the other

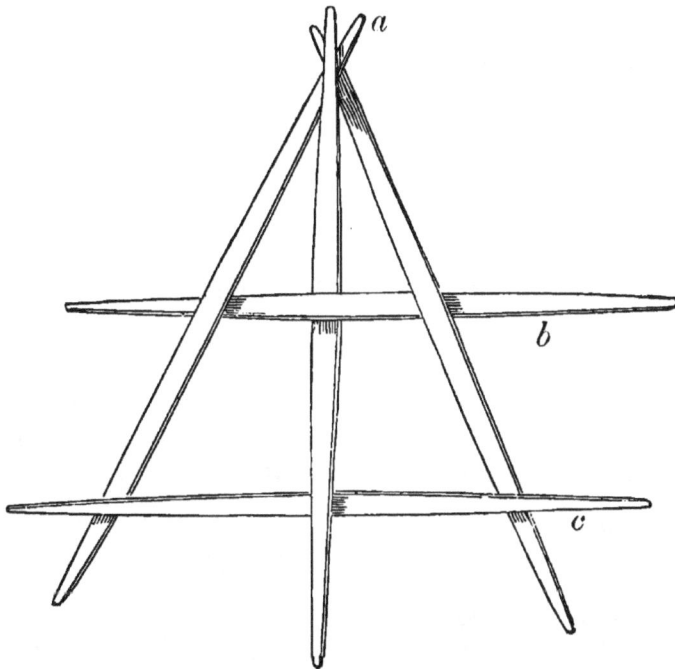

two successively, first *b*, then *c*. Now lay the figure upon any flat surface, letting the end *c* extend a short distance beyond the edge. If you touch a lighted match to *c*, in a moment each stick will leap into the air as if suddenly endowed with life and animation, quite unusual in such inert objects.

HOW TO CUT TOPS FROM GLASS BOTTLES.

A glass bottle when freed from its top can be utilized in many ways, and most boys will be glad to know how to get rid of this troublesome portion without smashing the whole thing into fragments.

A red-hot poker with a pointed end is the instrument used. First make a mark with a file to begin the cut; then apply the hot iron, and a crack will start, which will follow the iron wherever it is carried. This is, on the whole, simple, and better than the use of strings wet with turpentine, etc.

A BOY'S BAROMETER.

Take a common vial, or small bottle, cut off the rim by using the hot poker as directed above. Let the vial now be nearly filled with common rain water, and applying the finger to its mouth, turn it quickly upside down : on removing the finger it will be found that only a few drops will escape. Without a cork or stopper of any kind, the water will be retained within the bottle by the pressure of the external air, the weight of the air without the vial being so much greater than the small quantity within it. Now let a bit of tape be tied round the middle of the bottle, to which the two ends of a string may be attached, so as to form a loop to hang on a nail; let it be thus suspended in a perpendicular manner, with the mouth downward : and this is the barometer.

When the weather is fair, or inclined to be so, the

water will be level at its lower surface, or perhaps concave, like an individual butter plate turned upside down ;
but when disposed to be stormy, a drop will appear at the
mouth, which will enlarge till it falls, and then another
drop, so long as the humidity of the atmosphere continues.

AN INFALLIBLE BAROMETER.

With a few cents any boy can buy the chemicals required for this barometer, and obtain an instrument much
more reliable than many of the cheaper grades for sale in
the stores. Put two drams of pure nitrate of potash, and
half a dram of chloride of ammonium reduced to a powder,
into two ounces of pure alcohol, and place this mixture in
a clear glass bottle, covering the top with a piece of rubber or thin kid pierced with small holes.

If the weather is to be fine, the solid matters remain at
the bottom of the bottle, and the alcohol is as transparent
as usual. If rain is to fall in a short time, some of the
solid particles rise and fall in the alcohol, which becomes
somewhat thick and troubled. When a storm, tempest,
or even a squall is about to come on, all the solid matter
rises from the bottom of the bottle and forms a crust on
the surface of the alcohol which appears to be in a state
of fermentation. These appearances take place twenty-
four hours before the tempest ensues, and the point of the
horizon from which it is to blow is indicated by the particles gathering most on the side of the tube opposite to
that part whence the wind is to come. The longer the
diameter of the bottle the better for this kind of barometer.

THE BALANCING DOLL.

From a piece of soft wood whittle out a head and body like that in the illustration, making slits on either side for the insertion of the wings. These oar-shaped appendages are generally made from a shingle, and are affixed to the body by pressing them firmly into the slits. The whole thing can be painted to suit the fancy ; water colors spread on rather thickly answer quite as well for small objects of this class, if protected by a good coating of varnish, made by dissolving a few cents' worth of white shellac in a small quantity of alcohol. It is important that the oars are of the same weight and placed at equal angles with the body for this plaything to be successful.

THE BOOMERANG.

The boomerang is a weapon which has long been known as peculiar to the Australian savages, who are wonderfully skilled in its use.

It consists of an irregular shaped piece of hard wood, so constructed that by its aid, the unsuspecting game can be killed at an angle widely diverging from the line of direction in which it was thrown. Instances have been cited in which the boomerang, in the hands of these untutored savages, has accomplished wonderful feats. One of the favorite ways of throwing consists in sending the weapon in such a manner that it shall skim along just above the ground for about a hundred feet, then, rising in the air, double back upon its course, and hit a mark only a few feet in front of the thrower. Of course we do not expect to equal the savages in its use, when recent investigations show that it has taken the experience of generations upon generations of men and hundreds of years, to bring it to its present degree of excellence; but every boy may derive much fun from practicing with the little cardboard boomerang

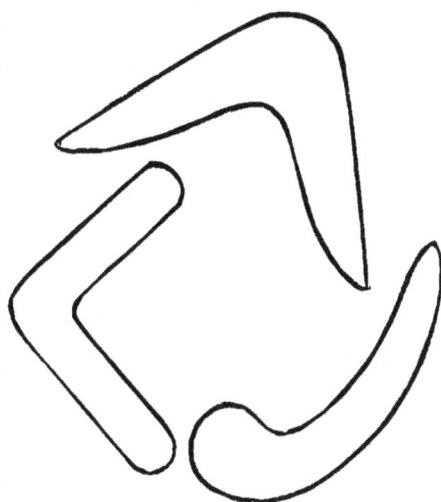

cut of stiff pasteboard in either of the forms given in the preceding page. To throw this, place it upon a book, one end extending beyond the edge; then, with a ruler or small stick, strike it forcibly upon the edge, and it will fly through the air and back again, in an amusing, lively manner, quite unlike any other missile in a boy's collection. It may be sent on its way by simply snapping it with the forefinger of the right hand while it is held on the book in your left. If you should try making one of wood to use out-of-doors, try it in the middle of a large open lot, for there is no telling what mischief it might do if it only had the chance.

THE MAGIC TELESCOPE.

The following, although requiring considerable skill in joining, can readily be made by any boy of fifteen, if he

is at all skillful in the use of carpenter's tools, and has a fair endowment of those two excellent qualities, patience and perseverance, so absolutely indispensable to success in almost any undertaking.

This telescope consists of a series of square wooden tubes, with an inside diameter of about five inches, so carefully joined together that no ray of light can find its way in through the crevices. The oblique lines are pieces of looking-glass, with their faces turned toward each other. Now, by placing the eye at *E*, of course it would seem that anything at *H* could be seen directly through the tubes *A B*, while if a book or other opaque object be interposed, as shown in Fig. 2, it would seem equally a matter of course that the view would be obstructed ; this, however, is not the case, as the mirrors reflect the object through the tube and it appears as plainly as when the book is removed.

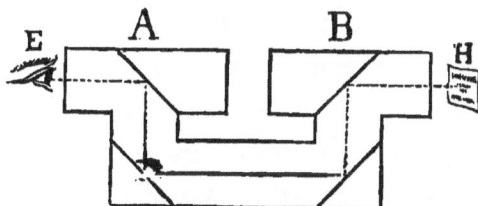

To those unfamiliar with its construction this magic telescope, by which you apparently see through a solid substance, is an unfailing source of wonder.

The object at *H* should be quite brilliantly lighted, as some of the rays are absorbed in the passage of the reflection through the tube ; especial care should also be taken to place the mirrors at a slant, exactly midway between the horizontal and the upright, or, to speak more scientifically, at an angle of 45 degrees to the line of the tubes.

The tubes *A* and *B* should not be so far apart at the place where the book is inserted as to permit the backs of the mirrors to be easily seen.

TO CRYSTALLIZE GRASSES, SEED-VESSELS, Etc.

Take a large-sized piece of alum, and pour over it a pint of boiling water, letting it stand until the water has taken up or dissolved all the alum it will. If at the end of a few hours any alum remains undissolved, you may be sure the water contains all the alum it can hold in a liquid state, and the solution is called a "saturated solution of alum."

During the summer, while the grasses are in their most perfect state, select such as you think will look well crystallized, and put them into a vase or wide-mouthed bottle to dry, being careful to spread them well apart, so that they may retain their perfect shape in drying. If the season of grasses should pass before you have a chance to collect them, the season of weeds is always at hand. Any boy, in his wanderings over marsh or mountain, through woods or our quiet village street, during even the coldest winter months, could not fail to see some beautiful sprays of seed-pods crowning many of our most common weeds, which if crystallized, would make a very pretty and acceptable present to mother for the corner bracket, or the shelf which seemed just a little bare before. Having secured your grasses or weeds, both together if you like, and having your saturated solution of alum at hand, lay as many tops of the grasses in a flat dish as will fill it without crowding, then pour the liquid over them, being careful that the parts you wish crystallized are under the surface. Let them lie in this position until well coated with the alum. When finished remove them and put in others. Continue in this manner until all are treated. If only a few crystals are desired they may be obtained by dipping the heads one at a time in the solution and slightly shaking them after each immersion. When all have been dipped, commence with the first and repeat the process. Do this until the crystals formed are as large as you wish them to be.

METHOD OF COLORING ALUM CRYSTALS.

In making these crystals the coloring should be added to the solution of alum in proportion to the shade which it is desired to produce. Coke, with a piece of lead attached to it in order to make it sink in the solution, is a good substance for a nucleus, if a cluster of crystals are to be formed. Any form, if wound around with knitting cotton, can be used, or the grasses above described can be dipped in these colored solutions, and very pretty results obtained.

Yellow: muriate of iron. Blue: solution of indigo in sulphuric acid. Pale blue: equal parts of alum and blue vitriol. Crimson: infusion of madder and cochineal. Black: Japan ink thickened with gum. Green: equal parts of alum and blue vitriol, with a few drops of sulphate of iron. Milk white: a crystal of alum held over a glass containing ammonia will become a milky white color upon its surface.

[NOTE.—To make an infusion of a substance you simply pour boiling water over it. The madder and cochineal are in the dry form, and only a little water should be used, as too much will make the color less brilliant.]

ANIMATED FIRE.

When small pieces of camphor are placed in a basin of pure water, a very peculiar motion commences; some of the pieces turn as if on an axis, others go steadily round the vessel, some seem to be pursuing others, and thus they continue forming a very curious and pleasing appearance; but if a single drop of sulphuric acid be put into the water, the motion of the camphor instantly stops. If a piece of camphor be lighted, and then carefully placed on the water, it burns with a bright flame, moving about with great rapidity, as if in search of something, but is instantly stopped by a drop of sulphuric acid.

A PRETTY ORNAMENT FOR A BOY TO MAKE.

Dissolve in seven different tumblers containing warm water, half ounces of sulphates of iron, copper, zinc, soda, alumina, magnesia, and potash. Pour them all, when completely dissolved, into a large flat dish, and stir the whole with a glass rod or bit of broken glass for a while. Place the dish in a warm place where it will be free from dust and will not be shaken. After due evaporation has taken place, the whole will begin to shoot out into crystals. These will be of various colors and forms, some little ones being gathered together in small groups, and other larger ones scattered throughout the whole fluid. By a little careful study you will soon be able to distinguish each crystal separately, from its peculiar form and color, thus learning an interesting lesson in chemistry, while making a beautiful ornament for your room. Be sure and preserve it carefully from the dust.

HOW TO MAKE A BLOWPIPE.

Procure two common clay pipes; break off the stem of one about three inches from the little end. Take a cork that exactly fits into the bowl of the other pipe, cut a hole through it large enough to insert the mouth-piece already broken off, and draw this through the opening till its larger end is even with the surface of the cork. Insert the cork in the bowl, and fill the end of the stem which touches the flame with a tiny ball of clay or chalk. Through this clay make a hole with a needle, and a blow-pipe is the result, which answers very well for any experiment a boy may be likely to try.

HOW TO BLOW GLASS.

Although it is impossible to give any detailed account of glass blowing which would be practicable for small boys, yet a child can amuse himself for hours, by simply melting bits of glass and joining them together; or by melting small glass tubes and drawing them out to mere threads; or again, blowing them up into tiny balloons until their surface is as thin as a soap bubble and almost as fragile. These little tubes are smaller than the end of a pipe-stem, about four inches long, and made of very thin glass. A dozen can be procured for ten or twelve cents at any place where chemical supplies are to be found. A short tallow candle, held in a cheap tin candle-stick, answers for the flame; and the tobacco-pipe, converted into the blowpipe just described, can be used in any of the experiments here given. Take a piece of a broken window pane, hold it in the left hand very near the candle flame, then holding the blowpipe so that the shorter end nearly touches the flame, blow steadily through the pipe-stem a current of air into the flame, which sends it upon the glass and soon reduces the part in contact with it to a red-hot melting mass; this can be worked into various shapes by forming it with the aid of pincers; or it can easily be joined to pieces of different colors, by holding the two together and turning the full force of the blaze upon them.

The little tubes may be heated in the same manner, and one end be closed air tight, by pinching it tightly while still hot; then, after heating the portion near the end to a red heat, lay the blowpipe aside, and, taking the tube away from the flame, blow into the open end with the mouth. If this is done quickly, before the glass has had time to cool, a pretty bubble or balloon is the result.

A SIPHON.

A simple glass siphon can be made by taking one of the above tubes and heating it at a point about one-third of its length from the end, till the surface appears a rosy

red ; then carefully bending it over the round part of a clothes-pin, till the two ends form parallel lines.

A simple experiment with the siphon affords consider-able amusement to the little folks, and is well worth try-ing. Take two tumblers, place them side by side, and fill one with water. Now fill the siphon with water and place the longer end in the empty tumbler, and the shorter one well down in the water of the other. Imme-diately the laborer will begin to work, pumping water into the empty vessel, and will not stop until he has re-duced the water in the full tumbler to a level with the end of the tube.

TO MELT STONES.

Many kinds of stones containing more or less metallic ores, can be readily melted by means of the blowpipe. When the specimens are small they can be placed upon a piece of mica, and then presented to the flame ; or a clay receptacle can be made for the purpose, by simply hol-lowing out a small cavity in one side of a lump of clay. Large ones can be held in the hand or with the pincers as in the case of the glass melting.

A SOAP BUBBLE.

Within the past few years soap-bubble parties have been quite the style among our young people, and not a few of the older members of society have joined in the frolic with as much zest as their younger competitors.

Usually at such gatherings, after the guests have all arrived, the hostess, having previously secured two or three boxes of bonbons, or other equally inexpensive trifles for prizes, presents each of her guests with an ordinary clay pipe, and leading the way to the room in which the bowls of soap-suds are already prepared, shows her prizes, and challenges all to the contest. If fine, large iridescent bubbles are desired, it is well to add a small quantity of glycerine to the water used. It is said that if the mixture of glycerine and water is allowed to stand some hours before it is used the effect is much better. Hot water and soap can be added just before the party enter, and only two bowls of the soap mixture are necessary for quite a large party. These should be placed upon small side tables or stands at opposite ends of the room. Two or three reliable persons should be chosen for judges to decide the contest. The parents or some older members of the family, at whose house the party is held, usually perform this duty. I should have added, when speaking of the soap mixture, that the common yellow soap intended for laundry use, is much better for this purpose than the finer toilet varieties most commonly used by amateur soap-bubble blowers.

RESIN BUBBLES.

If the end of a tobacco-pipe be dipped in melted resin, at a temperature a little above that of boiling water, taken out, and held nearly in a vertical position and blown through, bubbles will be formed of all possible sizes, from that of a hen's egg, down to sizes which can hardly be discerned by the naked eye, and from their silvery luster, and reflection of the different rays of light, they have a pleasing appearance. Some that have been formed these eight months, are as perfect as when first made. They generally assume the form of a string of beads, many of them perfectly regular, and connected by a very fine fiber, but the production is never twice alike. If expanded over a gas jet by means of a small rubber tube, they would probably float around the upper part of the room.

THE THREE MAGICAL CARDS.

Take three cards of the same size, and thick enough to

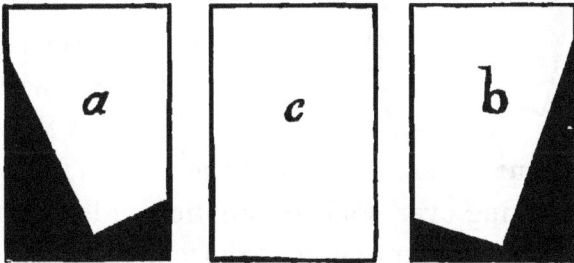

prevent the black surface from showing through; ink or paint over the whole of one side of *c*, having the other side perfectly white, and the others, *a* and *b*, in the parts shown in Fig. 1; they are now ready for use.

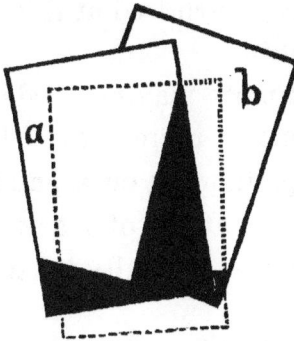

Fig. 2

Fig. 2 shows the first arrangement of them, *a* and *b* lapping over each other so that when *c* is placed in the

2

position shown by dotted lines the whole face presents a
perfectly white surface. Show this to your audience;
then, still holding them in sight, inform them in a neat
little speech, that by aid of some magic power you possess,
you can readily change these same cards to black, or back
again, at will.   Now holding them with their backs away
from you, in such a manner that the card *c* cannot be seen
by the other boys, turn them upside down and spread out
what were the lower parts of *a* and *b*. You have them
now in the position indicated
by Fig. 3, and after carefully
turning *c* you will find them
presenting a uniformly black
surface. Should any bit of
white show at the lower corner, cover it with your
thumb. When they are ar-
ranged to your satisfaction, hold them up in front of you,
and while saying over some cabalistic words, such as, for
instance, "Presto, agramento, calafesto—change!" blow
upon their faces and turn them around to your audience,
which will probably be greatly surprised at this undenia-
ble evidence of your magic skill.

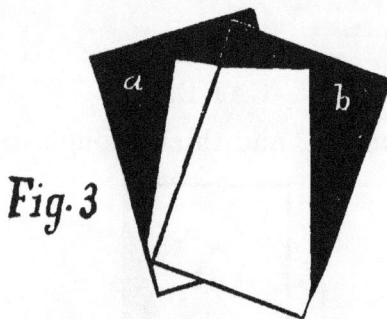

Fig. 3

    Instead of white, the ordinary playing cards may be
used, blacking the back of one to represent *c*. These are
much more showy than the plain white ones, and the trick
is not so easily discovered if slight bits of black are seen,
as those having black spots are generally taken for the
purpose.

    One day a little fellow who had been repeatedly mysti-

fied by this trick, saw the cards which his brother had prepared lying on the table. He took them up, examined them carefully for a moment, then, with his little face all aglow at the revelation, he exclaimed, "Ha! I've found out how you do it now, you just blow charcoal on the other part." How he got rid of the part already black, he did not explain, nor did we think to ask him, but he had at last solved the puzzle of their turning black, and that was all he cared to do at the time.

AN OPTICAL GAME.

Hold a ring between thumb and forefinger at some distance from the boy addressed, and giving him a crooked stick, ask him to close one eye and try to catch the ring on the stick. This game looks so very simple, that any boy is certain he can do it at one thrust, and is only made aware of its difficulties after several unsuccessful attempts.

TO TELL THE NUMBER THOUGHT OF BY A PERSON.

Desire the person who has thought of a number to triple it, and to take the exact half of that; triple that half if the number was even, or if odd multiply the larger half by 3; and ask him how many times that answer contains nine: for the answer will contain the double of that number of nines, and one more if it be odd. Thus if the number thought of is 5, its triple will be 15, which cannot be

divided by 2 without a remainder. The greater half of
15 is 8. If we multiply this by 3 we have 24, which contains 9 twice. So we shall have $2 + 2 + 1 = 5$, the number first thought of.

THE COUNTER PUZZLE.

In an old book published over half a century ago, I
came across this puzzle; and finding it gave an evening's
entertainment to our young folks, I introduce it here for
the benefit of those boys who take especial delight in
games of an arithmetical nature.

Out of thin cardboard—old business cards answer this
purpose nicely—make thirty-two blank counters, the size
of a dime. Then upon a piece of note-paper mark off a
figure just three inches square, and divide it by lines into
nine compartments, each containing one square inch.
The puzzle is, to arrange the counters in the external cells
of the square four different times, and each time to have
nine in a row, yet to have the sum of the counters different, and varying from twenty to thirty-two. If you will
inspect the following figures you will see how this is pos-

Fig. 1

3	3	3
3		3
3	3	3

2

4	1	4
1		1
4	1	4

3

2	5	2
5		5
2	5	2

sible: the first represents the original disposition of the

counters in the cells of the square; the second, that of the same counters when four are taken away; the third, the manner in which they must be disposed when these four are brought back with four others; and the fourth with the addition of four more. There are always nine in each external row, and yet in the first case the whole number is twenty-four, in the second it is twenty, in the third twenty-eight, and in the fourth thirty-two. The numbers are substituted in the place of the counters in the above figures for convenience, but Fig. 5 represents the disposition of the counters, as indicated in Fig. 2.

4

1	7	1
7		7
1	7	1

5

ANOTHER ARITHMETICAL TRICK.

By knowing the last figure of the product of any two numbers, to tell the other figures. If the number seventy-three be multiplied by each of the numbers in the following arithmetical progression, 3, 6, 9, 12, 15, 18, 21, 24, 27, the products will terminate with the nine digits, in this order, 9, 8, 7, 6, 5, 4, 3, 2, 1; the numbers themselves being as follows: 219, 438, 657, 876, 1095, 1314, 1533, 1752, and 1971. Let, therefore, a little bag be provided, consisting of two partitions, into one of which put several tickets, marked with the number 73, and into the other put as many tickets, 3, 6, 9, etc., up to 27. Then open that part of the bag containing the number 73, and ask a person to take out one ticket only ; after which, dexterously change the opening, and desire another person to take a ticket from the other part. Let them now multiply their two numbers together, and tell you the last figure of the product, by which you will readily determine from the foregoing series what the remaining figures must be. Suppose, for example, the numbers taken out of the bag were 73 and 12, then as the product of these two numbers, which is 876, has 6 for its last figure, you will readily know it is the fourth of the series and the other two figures must be 8 and 7.

TO TELL TWO OR MORE NUMBERS WHICH A PERSON HAS THOUGHT OF.

These numbers must not exceed 9. Let him think of two or three numbers, double the first and add 1 to the product, multiply the whole by 5, and add to that product the second number. If there be a third, make him double the first sum and add 1 to it ; then desire him to multiply the new sum by 5, and to add to it the third number. If there should be a fourth number, you must proceed in the same manner, desiring him to double the preceding sum, to add 1 to it, to multiply by 5, and then to add the fourth number, and so on. Then ask the number arising from the addition of the last number thought of, and if there were two numbers subtract 5 from it : if three, 55 ; if four, 555, and so on, for the remainder will be composed of figures, of which the first on the left will be the first number thought of, the next the second, and so of the rest.

Suppose the numbers thought of to be 3, 4, 6 ; by adding 1 to 6, the double of the first, we have 7, which being multiplied by 5 gives 35 ; if 4, the second number thought of, be then added, we shall have 39, which doubled gives 78, and if we add 1, and multiply 79 by 5, the result will be 395. Lastly, if we add 6, the third number thought of, the sum will be 401, and if 55 be deducted from it we shall have for the remainder 346, the figures of which 3, 4, and 6, indicate in order the three numbers thought of.

AN EASY PROOF FOR SUMS IN MULTIPLICATION.

As boys are always interested in short cuts in arithmetical processes, it may be well to insert for the benefit of those who are studying multiplication, a method of proving their examples which I learned a short time ago from an old banker of New York. This rule is simply to add the digits of both multiplicand and multiplier, divide both answers by 9, and multiply the remainders ; divide this product by 9 and the remainder will be, if the example is correct, the same as that obtained by adding the digits of the product and dividing that answer by 9. For instance, suppose after multiplying 4359 by 2786 we have 12144174 for the answer ; now instead of performing this operation over a second time to make sure our answer is correct, we simply add the digits in 4359 and divide the sum 21 by 9, we find we have 3 left. As it is the only remainder we have to deal with, we need not keep the other figures. By adding the digits in the multiplier we obtain 23, which divided by 9 gives 2 and 5 remainder. Now, multiplying the first remainder by the second we have 15 : this product divided by 9 gives 1 and 6 remainder. If the product 12144174 is correct, the sum of its digits divided by 9 will leave 6 for a remainder. Performing the operation, we find the sum of its digits is 24, divided by 9 equals 2 and 6 remainder. As both the remainders correspond, the answer was correct. After a little practice you will find you can prove your examples very quickly by this method, and where a number of sums are given without the answers it will be of invaluable assistance, besides saving you a great amount of labor.

THE SELF-RECTIFYING DART.

The dart, and its larger brother the javelin, were among the earliest weapons used in warfare, and were very skilfully thrown, not only by the Roman soldiers, but by the Goths and other savage tribes who lived in the regions north of them.

These javelins were large affairs, measuring some six or seven feet in length ; the handle, a tough piece of wood, was generally four and one-half feet in length, and an inch in diameter, while the rest of the length was taken up by the barbed triangular-shaped head.

Ever since those days children of all nations and climes

have made toy implements, resembling those in general appearance, but varying much in size and materials used.

The little dart described below is perhaps the tiniest and least formidable of them all; but even this should not be carelessly tossed about the room in which others are playing; when, however, thrown in the open air, and away from others who might be hurt, there is considerable amusement derived from the airy bit of flying wood, which always comes down with such unerring certainty upon its spear-like head. To make this dart, take half a sheet of note-paper, double it diagonally across, so that its top edge may fall evenly upon that of one side (see Fig. 1), and cut off the surplus piece of paper which remains uncovered at the bottom of the page. Open your square, and fold it again in the other diagonal line *c, d* (the first is represented on Fig. 2, as *a, b*). Now, opening again, fold upon the line *e, f*, then, after opening, upon *g, h*. Crease all the folds as you make them. Now, having prepared your handle, which consists of a piece of wood about 8 inches long and the size of a lead pencil, cut across one end at right angles, with slits nearly or quite an inch in depth; take your paper and open it flat once more. Fold the diagonals so that the four points, *a, b, c, d*, shall all meet together above *x*, and the

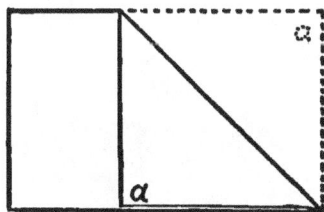

Fig. 1

lines *ax*, *bx*, *cx*, and *dx* shall meet at the central line of the figure, and the four shorter lines, *ex*, *fx*, etc., form the outside edges of the figure. Insert a tiny wedge or knife-blade at the bottom of the slits, and press the paper down in the opening, bringing the folded edges through each of the four slits ; remove the wedge, and the paper will be firmly held in its place. Insert a needle or headless pin in the other end of the wood, and the dart is ready for use.

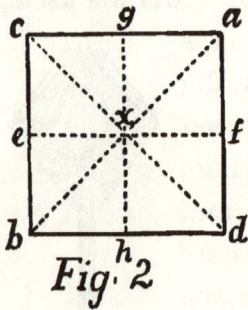

Fig. 2

THE BALANCING PIN.

This amusing feat I first saw performed in our little district school-house, many years ago.

One morning, while the teacher was busy with his class at the blackboard, one of the boys drew an old clay pipe-stem from his pocket, and producing a small green gooseberry and a pin from some other part of his clothing, gave us boys to understand that he was about to perform some wonderful trick with them. We were of course all attention, and as the teacher's back re-

mained turned toward us, he proceeded to astonish us with his remarkable feat. He first stuck the pin through the gooseberry, and then let it fall, point downward, into one end of the pipe-stem; then, placing the other end to his mouth, and holding his head thrown well over backward, he blew into the opening, and the gooseberry and pin arose quite clear of the tube, and began dancing and balancing above it in a very funny way. How long it would have continued its gyrations I cannot tell, probably until his breath gave out, but just then a little boy in the front row made some exclamation, and straightway the teacher's head came around, the pipe-stem, pin, and gooseberry went on a voyage of discovery out of the school-house window, and the boy got a thrashing for his pains. But the feat was often performed by us all after that, and some years later, when a second generation of boys were having over again the tricks and sports their older brothers had outgrown, I saw the same principle applied under more favorable conditions. Instead of the straight pipe-stem, which necessitated throwing the head over backward, to insure its perpendicular position, a tube bent at a right angle near one end was used, and the balancing of the pin could be much more easily watched by the performer. Instead of the gooseberry, a currant, pea, or any light, round fruit can be substituted, and a small glass tube may take the place of the pipe-stem.

A BOX-SLED FOR BABY.

Procure a deep, smooth soap-box, and decide how high you wish the back and front to be; then take a piece of brown paper, the exact size of the sides of the box, and mark on it a curve, which shall unite the high back with the low front. After this has assumed a perfectly satisfactory form, cut it out and tack it on one side of the box. Mark the outline carefully on both side-pieces, and saw the boards as indicated by the line; cut the front straight across, and rasp and sand-paper the edges till they are very smooth and well rounded. Next paint the box inside and out, excepting the bottom, which is to be fastened to the sled, with a thick coat of burnt umber, and give it a good drying. Then with light-blue paint, make a narrow band, one-fourth of an inch wide, entirely around each side, the back, and the front, about half an inch from the edge. Stencil a pretty design on the back, and the name of the little owner on each side; let this thoroughly dry, and finish with two coats of varnish. A little seat can be fitted in the back part if desired, but a pillow answers the purpose much better.

A SET OF CARS.

Procure a stick of wood of any length, and an inch and a half square at the ends. Saw it into pieces six inches in length, being careful to cut it evenly, that the blocks may be rectangular in form. Round off the tops slightly at the edges and paint them brown, then give the sides and ends a good coating of yellow.

If you have no oil paints, it would be a good investment to get a few tubes, as they are not expensive, and are of invaluable assistance in adding beauty and naturalness to many things a boy can make. For the cars, a tube of chrome yellow, one of Indian-red, and one of black would

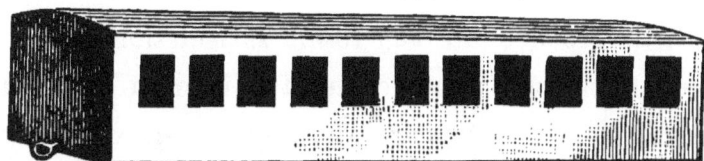

be needed, but as those are not over seven or eight cents apiece the whole cost would be small. The windows can perhaps be most conveniently put on by "stencilling." To do this, cut a piece of stout paper or thin cardboard the exact size of the side of the car, and mark the windows on it in their proper places (see Fig. 2). Then cut out the windows thus drawn with the point of a sharp penknife. Catch the card firmly upon the surface by driving two or three fine pins through it into the wood. Finally, with your brush moderately filled with the black paint, cover all the yellow surface exposed through the openings; then remove the card very carefully and one side of your car will be complete. After painting the whole set, another long time will be needed for drying. During the meantime obtain a few screw-eyes and hooks, and, when perfectly dry, screw a hook into the left and an eye into the right end of each car, join them into a train, and you will find you have a strong set of cars with which your little brother can play to his satisfaction, without a fear of breaking. The locomotive is more difficult to make, but with a little care any boy of ten can be quite certain of success.

THE TOY LOCOMOTIVE.

The thin ends of a common soap-box afford very good

Fig. 1

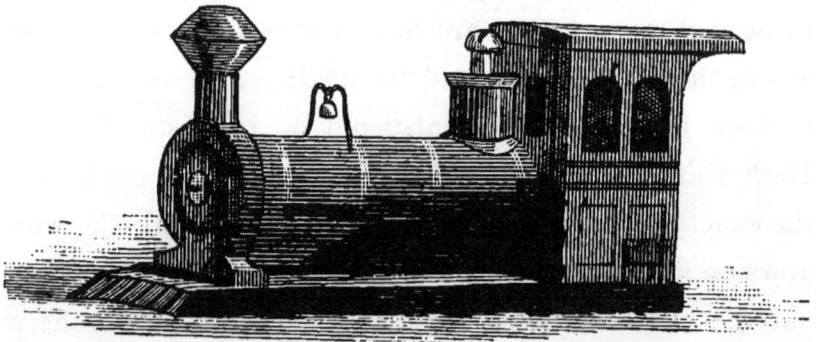

material for the base of this locomotive, while the end of

a curtain-roller makes a capital boiler. The cab can be cut from a cigar-box, and a button-mold will do for the boiler-head. First cut from the thicker wood a base in shape like Fig. 1, and seven inches long by one and a half wide;

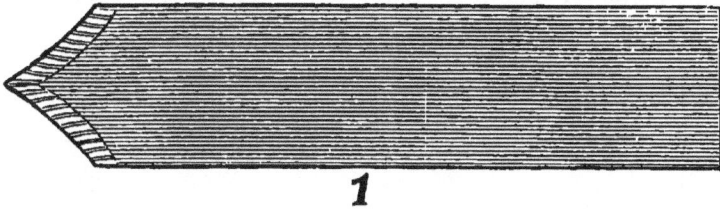

1

with a jackknife bevel it on either side of the pointed end to correspond to the shape of the pilot, as shown in the cut. Saw the roller even at either end just four inches in length. Next cut from a solid block of wood a smoke-stack three inches high and an inch in diameter across the top. The cab is cut from the cigar-box wood, and consists of a front like *a*, two side-pieces like *b*, and a top like that seen in Fig. 1; round off the edges of the top to give it a slightly convex surface like the tops of the cars. Now, with brads, fasten these three parts together. Then with a long, slender brass screw fasten the button-mold and smoke-stack on front of the boiler. The screw should have as large a head as it is possible to find, and should be long enough to extend half an inch or more into the round section of wood or boiler. Cover

the whole, excepting the cab, with two thick coats of black paint, being careful that the first is perfectly dry before the second is put on. After the blackened surface is thoroughly dry and hard, put the red stripes on the pilot, as seen in the cut : and for the brass bands around the boiler use chrome yellow. The cab is painted Indian-red, and after this is perfectly dry, the windows are painted on with black, as in the cars.

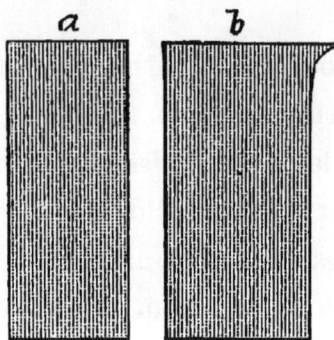

The little ornamental lines on the cab are made with the yellow paint. A large round-headed brass screw driven through a low flat spool (such as is used for button-hole twist), into the top of the boiler in front of the cab, makes a good steam-chest and whistle, and adds the finishing touch to this indestructible little toy. If you anticipate making this train of cars for a Christmas present, begin it in time, as paint dries much more slowly in winter than in summer, and it is absolutely necessary that each coat be perfectly dry before the next is applied. Varnishing greatly improves the durability and appearance of the painted surface. Shellac dissolved in alcohol makes the best varnish for this kind of work. It should be made moderately thick, and if intended for light-colored work, white shellac should be used, as the dark leaves a slight stain upon the surface. I forgot to add in its proper place that a brass button, caught in on top by a stiff wire, is made to represent a bell. The wire should be first bent into the shape seen in the illustration; the button then hung in position, and the wire finally driven into the holes made to receive it.

The tender consists of a piece of wood the same width but only half the length of one of the cars, and one inch high. This is painted black with a narrow band of yellow running around the sides near the top, and is fastened to the locomotive and car by means of the screw-eye and hook.

A FREIGHT TRAIN.

The locomotive for this train can be made like the one already described, and the cars are cut from a rectangular stick, in the same manner as the passenger cars. These should receive a thick coat of Indian-red paint, and if this does not cover well, that is, if any of the wood shows through, another coat should be given. After the paint is perfectly dry, put on one edge of the side, near the top, a number in white, and two or three letters in the same color, to represent the sides of the freight cars on different lines.   If desired, the cars can be painted different colors, and the side decorations copied from the car you mean to represent.   Give the whole a good varnishing with the shellac dissolved in alcohol, and allow plenty of time to elapse before the toy is used, for it to become perfectly dry and hard.

A LOT OF PAPER WINDMILLS.

Take a thin stick of wood a foot and a half or two feet long, and nail to it four cross-pieces, graduated in length and six or seven inches apart.   The shorter, at the top, should measure about six inches.   Cut out of stiff, colored

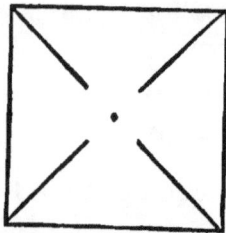

paper (the greater the variety the prettier the effect) fifteen pieces, each three inches square, and slit each piece as indicated by the diagonal lines in the figure.   Out of pretty tissue-paper cut three round pieces for each mill,

about the size of a silver dollar, and with a dull knife
scrape their edges, that they may slightly curl like the
petals of a rose; crinkle them at the center if intended
for a rose, or from the edge toward the center if for
asters or marigolds, and thrust a large, strong pin through
the middle of each disk, drawing the flower well down
over the head ; then, bending the opposite corners of each

square of paper so that they shall all rest over the central
dot marked on each (Fig. 1), force the pin with the flower
on its head, down through the five thicknesses of paper,
driving it well into the wood of the frame. In doing this
care should be taken to avoid creasing the curved edges
of the windmills. They are placed upon the frame-work
as indicated in the cut.

Very pretty windmills are often made of only two shades, common note-paper being used for the wheels, and a bright, rosy pink tissue-paper for the flowers. Indeed, those made of common brown wrapping-paper without any flowers at all give more satisfaction in a light wind than the more elaborate ones described above.

A WINTER GARDEN.

Most boys love flowers; and many families, especially in the country, would keep more through the winter than they do, if they had the space and time to devote to them, necessary for their preservation. A number of pots, sufficiently large to hold good-sized plants, take up considerable room; and no little time is required each day, to keep the pots clean and the plants well watered. Now, boys, I have a suggestion to make, which I intend for your ears alone. Why can't you make a winter garden, and, if necessary, take care of it through the season? It will amply repay you for your labor, and do much toward brightening the home life through the long dreary months, when everything without is covered with ice and snow.

First procure a soap-box, the best and tightest you can find: if any cracks are too wide to be easily closed with putty, nail laths over them on the inside, line their edges, and, in fact, stop every seam and crevice with good thick layers of putty. Next paint over the entire inside with any colored pigment you may have, as it does not show when the box is filled with earth, but simply aids in making it water-tight.

Now take four strong pieces of wood, about two and a half feet long ; smooth them well and sand-paper ; be sure both ends are cut off evenly, and that each leg is the same length as the other three, and, finally, nail them firmly to the four corners of the box, letting the tops come in line with its upper edge, and give the whole thing two good coats of Indian-red. A very pretty stand is made by substituting the straight trunks of young forest trees with their bark left on in place of the smooth, painted legs ; bore holes in the bottom of the legs and insert casters, and finish by giving the entire outer surface a thick coating of varnish. Then get a good wheelbarrow-load of fine leaf-mold, about half that quantity of sand, and some common garden soil. Stir these well together, and fill the box half full with the mixture, first covering the bottom with pebbles, to secure drainage. Before this, however, bore a hole with a good-sized gimlet in the bottom of the box, and fit a soft pine peg to close it from the under side. When the plants are watered this peg can be removed, and a dish placed beneath the opening to catch the surplus water.

You are now ready for the plants. I find almost any garden plants thrive well in this box, so any favorites you may have will soon make themselves at home in these new quarters. It is well to put vines around the edge, as they fall over, and their glossy green leaves and stems form an agreeable contrast to the dark-red background of the box itself. In my present winter garden I have German and Cenilworth ivy, partridge-berry, and the common inch-plant for vines. In the center is a large salvia, taken up so carefully that the great ball of dirt was not shaken from its roots. On one side is a calla lily, and on the other a feverfew of the large double variety. At the ends are fuchsias and heliotrope, and scattered over the other available spots are verbenas and petunias, sweet peas and lobelia ; one or two fish-geraniums of bright colors also found a place, and a little wood-violet nestled in one corner has bloomed since early spring. A beautiful large purple pansy, too, has been blooming all winter in another corner of the box.

Over this garden are two hanging-pots, one filled with pink oxalis, and the other with a Chinese pink ; both have contributed their full share of blossoms during the entire season, and neither seems to tire of well-doing. I must now tell you how to care for these beautiful pets, for they must receive some attention, which, however, is very small when compared with that required by their sisters in pots. First, always water them with warm water (almost as hot as you can bear your hand in), pour this around the roots in sufficient quantities to thoroughly moisten the soil. A good rule to be observed in watering your plants is to pour on the water until it begins to run out of the hole in the bottom of the box. With such thorough wetting down they will not need water oftener than twice a week, except when the sun is very hot, and the moisture evaporates quickly. A little carbonate of ammonia added to the water greatly improves their growth, and half-a-dozen grains of permanganate of potash added once a fortnight to the warm bath turns their foliage a rich dark green. With a whisk broom, sprinkle them once or twice a week with water which is also warm, but not as hot as that used on their roots ; this operation takes but little time, scarcely five minutes, and as the stand is on casters it can be easily moved to the middle of the room, and each side can then receive its full share of the washing. It is safe to predict that if any boy would make the stand, and supply it with rich soil, his mother or some one of his sisters would only be too happy to plant and care for the flowers it might hold.

THE BOOT PUZZLE.

First take a piece of paper, double it, and cut from it a pair of boots, the fold in the paper coming at the top of the boots, and consequently joining them together. Then

take another piece, fold it and cut it in the form of Fig.
2, *a* being the folded end.   Fold still another piece and

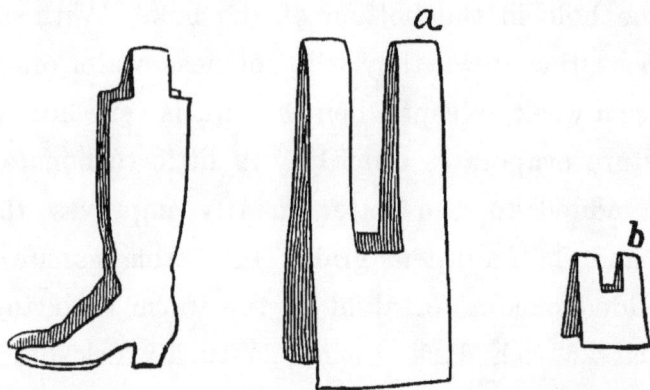

Fig. 1   Fig. 2   Fig. 3

cut it like Fig. 3, *b* representing the folding side.   Now
open the smaller piece, as in Fig. 4, and push the point *a*

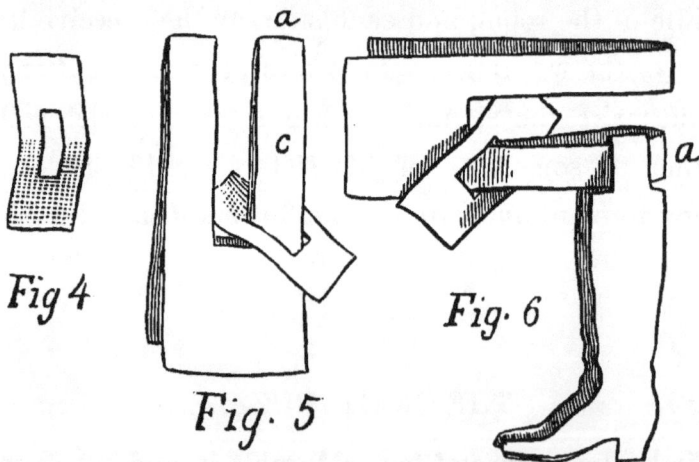

Fig 4

Fig. 5

Fig. 6

through the opening in its center (Fig. 5).   Then put one
boot through the loop of the long arm, *c*, between *a* and

the smaller piece, which has been pushed forward as far as it will go (Fig. 6). Now pull the smaller piece down over *a*, and open the largest piece, and the boots are fastened on to the larger paper in such a way that it is rather hard for the uninitiated to extricate them.

After they are fastened in place, with your finger-nail smooth out the creases made at *a*, Fig. 5, as their appear-

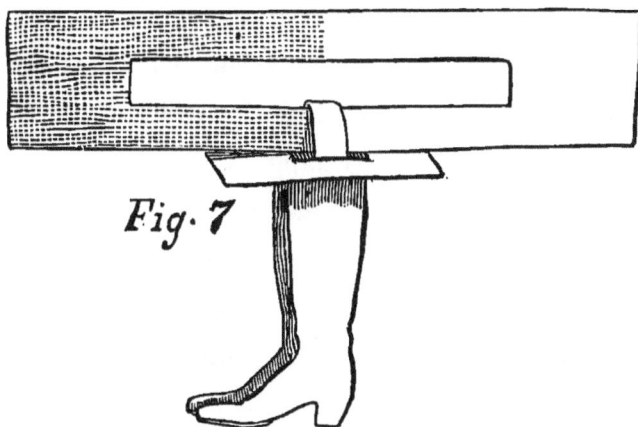

Fig. 7

ance might furnish a clue toward solving the mystery. It is best when cutting Fig. 2 to avoid the creasing if possible.

When you pass them to your friends to take off, explain that they are not to bend the boots. It is an excellent plan to make the last-named articles of cardboard, while the other parts are simply of note-paper.

HOW TO TAKE PORTRAITS.

The person whose portrait is to be taken must sit so that his shadow is thrown upon a sheet of cardboard or thick white paper placed against the wall. To obtain a sharp outline there should be a fixed distance between the lamp, wall, and sitter, which can easily be found by experiment. The sitter must keep perfectly still while the outline of the shadow is quickly traced upon the paper. A tumbler or roll of paper may be placed between the head of the sitter and the wall, to aid in holding the head quiet. The tracing is then cut out with a pair of scissors or a sharp penknife, and placed upon a dark cloth or paper. This is a very pleasing amusement for a cold winter's evening, and the results are often profile likenesses not only very striking but often wonderfully accurate.

HOW TO BREAK A STRING.

No boy feels himself perfectly at home if he has not one pocket at least full of strings, and a good sharp jackknife at his command. Although the jackknife often gets lost, the string is usually at hand, and most boys will probably be glad to learn how a good strong cord can be broken without injury to the hands. Take the cord and

pass it around the left hand, as shown in Fig. A, so as
to form a cross or double loop over the palm. One end

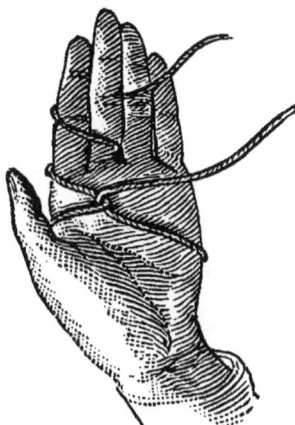

is then wound round the fingers, and the other seized
in the right hand. Then, by closing both hands, and

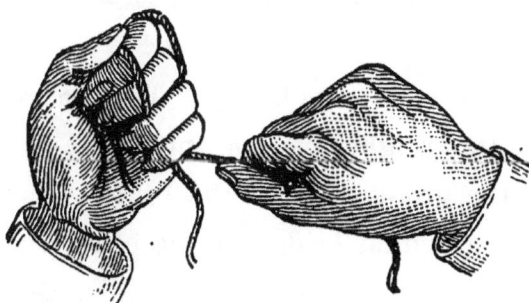

giving a very sharp, quick pull, the string will be broken
at the cross in the left hand.

For those boys living in the country who have a musical turn, but have never seen this little instrument, I write the following description of

A CORN-STALK FIDDLE.

Find a good straight corn-stalk, and with your jack-knife cut four slits from joint to joint, as seen in the upper figure. Then from a bit of wood cut a bridge, as shown just below. With the point of the knife lift the

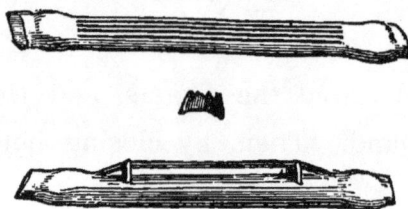

three strings and insert the bridge. Then carefully raise the bridge to its upright position, spread the strings until they rest in the grooves cut in the bridge for that purpose, and put a similar bridge at the other end. Make the bow in the same manner, of a smaller section of a stalk, and the instrument is complete. I have never heard a very decided tune played on this fiddle, but perhaps some of my readers may be able to get music from this simple little instrument.

THE XYLOPHONE.

The xylophone is an instrument of great antiquity, having been used in a slightly different form by both Greeks and Hebrews. It is now sometimes used in connection with other instruments in our larger orchestras, in which case, however, the bars are usually made of metal. Its construction is very simple, and any boy having a good ear for music can readily make one.

The instrument is composed of strips of wood of various sizes, and thick enough to allow the passage of a stout piece of twine or fish-line, as seen in the illustration. The largest strips give the lowest notes. The first note of the scale may be a strip of any convenient size, and the succeeding strips are tuned by carefully cutting away from

the under side until the desired tone is produced. They
are strung upon cords, in the manner shown in Fig. 2, a
knot being made on each side to keep the strip in place;
and finally, across the upper part of a box, in order to
give sufficient resonance of sound. In putting these strips
together, it is necessary to have the holes through which

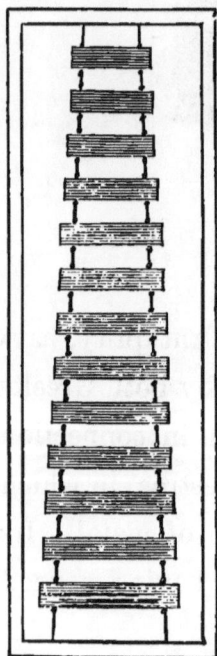

Fig. 3

Fig. 2

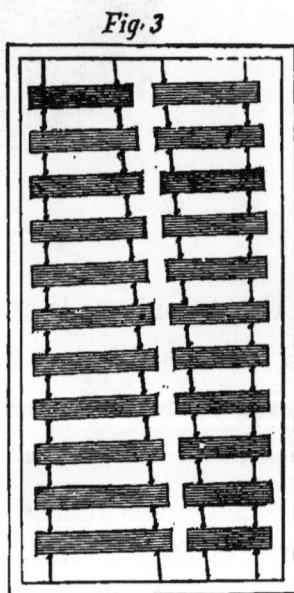

they are strung at a slight angle, or in the direction of
the slant which the strings take when fastened to the
frame.

The arrangement seen in Fig. 3 is perhaps best adapted
to the usual form of a box, and affords a greater range of

notes. It would be well to letter the upper part of the bars with the name of the note they are intended to produce, and the wood should be thoroughly seasoned from which these bars are made.

It is well to have the lowest note not the first of the scale but a fifth below, and the highest three or four notes above the octave. This will give sufficient compass for any-air you may care to play.

A good ear for music is of the greatest importance to insure success in constructing an instrument of this description, and it would simply be a waste of time and patience for any boy not so blessed, to venture upon the undertaking.

Little wooden mallets are sometimes used to play upon this xylophone, but the little drumsticks belonging to the common toy drum are better for the purpose.

Among the tribes of southern Africa an instrument of this class holds the chief place in their festivals, and is played upon with considerable skill by many of their native musicians. This piano, called by them "marimba," consists of two bars of wood placed side by side; in the most southern portions quite straight, but farther north, bent round so as to resemble half the tire of a carriage-wheel; across these are placed about fifteen wooden keys, each of which is two or three inches broad, and fifteen or eighteen inches long, and their thickness, as in the case of the xylophone, is regulated according to the deepness of the note required. Each of the keys has a calabash beneath it; from the upper part of each a portion is cut off to enable them to embrace the bars, and form hollow sounding-boards to the keys, which also are of different sizes, according to the note required; and little drumsticks, like those spoken of above, elicit the music. Rapidity of execution seems much admired among them, and the music is pleasant to the ear.

In Angola, the Portuguese use the marimba in their dances.

THE ÆOLIAN HARP.

This simple little musical instrument derives its name from Æolus, god of the winds, who is said to have lived

at Stromboli, then called Strongyle, while he reigned over
the Æolian islands, just north of Sicily. His island was
entirely surrounded by a wall of brass, and by perfectly
smooth precipitous rocks. Here he dwelt in continual
joy and festivity with his wife and children ; the latter,
six sons and as many daughters, are said to be a poetic
type of the twelve months of the year. And here he kept
the winds, tied up in bags, in perfect subjection, only let-

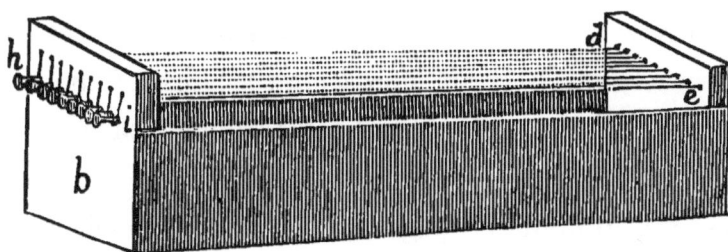

ting them out when called upon to do so by Neptune, god
of the sea. As the winds served Æolus on his little isle, so
we force them to serve us in our far-away western homes,
by operating upon our instrument and making music to
soothe and calm us when we are too tired or indolent to
make it for ourselves. The simplest form this instrument
can have is a single string of strong waxed silk, stretched
between two bits of wood, inserted under the lower win-
dow-sash, sufficient space being allowed between the win-
dow-sill and the sash for the vibration of the string.

The other and more satisfactory harp is made like that

in the engraving, and is not so difficult an undertaking, that any boy who can handle carpenter's tools need fear to try it. Take two long strips of thin, soft pine wood, four and five inches wide respectively, and a little shorter than the sash is wide, to allow for the length of the pegs at one end; then from common seven-eighths of an inch board make two other pieces in shape like *b*, six inches wide, six high, on the narrower, and seven on the back or longer side. With a small gimlet make in both ends a row of eight or nine holes, at equal distances from each other, and half an inch from the edge of the slanting top, for the strings to pass through; then with a larger gimlet bore in one end only, the second row of holes, *h i*, to hold the pegs upon which the ends of the strings are to be wound. Nail the parts together as in the cut, making the lower edges of the pieces meet at the bottom; then from the outside of *d e* draw through as many pieces of violin string (the smallest or E string) as you have holes in your wood. Hold these by knots on the outside, and having brought them across the box pass them through the corresponding holes in the other end, and twist them around the pegs below, in the same manner that the strings are fastened in the violin itself. Unlike the violin, however, these should not be drawn too tight, simply stretched evenly across, and must all be tuned in unison. That is, having drawn one as tight as you think best, draw the others, one at a time, till they give forth the same musical note when snapped with the finger. Now put another thin piece of board across the top which shall just cover it like the lid of a desk. This was purposely left out in the illustration, that the arrangement of the strings might be more fully seen, but is necessary in the complete instrument. If catgut cannot be readily obtained, strong pieces of sadlers' silk, well waxed, may be used in its place, although the tones resulting are not as musical, or the strains as soft and lulling in character, as those produced by the former.

After the instrument is properly tuned, place it upon the ledge of an open window, and let the sash down upon it, when, if there is any breeze stirring, it will pour forth strains of sweet, drowsy music, beautifully described by the poet Thomson, as supplying the most suitable harmonies for the *Castle of Indolence.*

THE BOSTON CLAPPER.

Take a piece of soft wood, five or six inches long, and whittle out of one end a hollow box, open at the top and outer end, like that represented in the illustration. Cut a groove around the inside, near the top, for the cover to slide in. Make this cover of a very thin piece of tough wood, and one-third as long as the opening, pushing it, when completed, well up against the inner end of the box; see *b*, in the figure, for size and position of cover.

The handle, *f*, is simply for convenience in holding the instrument. Pass a piece of strong string or fish-line twice around the box at the point *d*, and after drawing it as tightly as possible, tie it firmly on the under side.

Out of hard, tough wood make a thin, slender tongue,

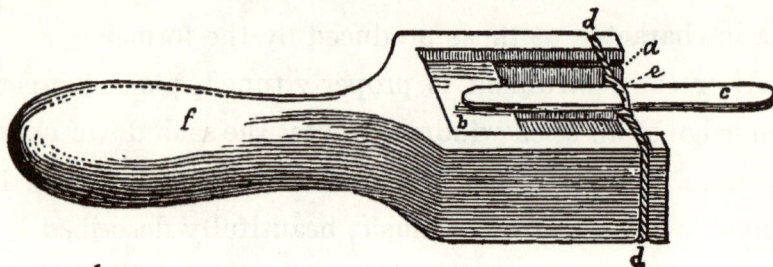

c, and place this between the two strings at *e*. Now twist this tongue over and over, each time drawing out the longer end, to allow of the other sliding by the edge of the cover. At each revolution of *c* the string is twisted tighter around the box, and if the end of *c* is touched, the other end strikes with more force upon the cover *b*.

When sufficiently tight, grasp the handle with your left hand, and having the point well over the cover, commence with the third finger of your right hand and strike down on the end *c* with the fingers in their order, giving quick and repeated blows, like the successive taps of a drum. The music produced, if not strictly melodious, is quite enchanting to the average American schoolboy.

PAPIER-MACHÉ.

I have now come to one of the most fascinating and at the same time useful employments a boy can have ; one which not only affords amusement for the time being, but, if properly executed, furnishes home with much which is useful or ornamental, at scarcely any expense beyond the mere time and labor consumed in the work.

How many of my readers know how to make things of papier-maché? None who are old enough to read these directions are too young to make really useful objects or pretty playthings of this inexpensive medium ; indeed, many of the children of India, Persia, and many other Asiatic countries support themselves, and in some instances whole families, by making ornaments of papier-maché.

In Germany this art is carried to a great extent, and a large proportion of the German toys so common in our stores, as well as the jointed bodies of the expensive French and German dolls, are made of this material.

Papier-maché means " softened paper," and is simply

any old soft paper converted into pulp by water; the poorer the paper the better. Cheap newspapers, such as tear with a mere touch, thin handbills and posters, are all particularly suited for this purpose.

For a first trial it would be well to take some simple object, and a cup would perhaps make as good a beginning as any. First have some good flour-paste made, by pouring into boiling water enough flour, which has previously been moistened with cold water, to make a substance rather thicker than boiled starch; this should be stirred only enough to unite the flour with the water, and to prevent burning. Add to this one or two old newspapers and a dish of water, a broad brush for the paste, and any prettily shaped tea-cup conveniently at hand, and you have all the materials required. A bag filled with sand or stuffed hard with cotton is a great help in molding, although not indispensable to the operation. Take the cup, which should be well smeared over with sweet-oil or lard, and cutting out a piece of paper sufficiently large, wet it, and press it down on the cup, using the fingers, or the sand bag, if you have it, for the purpose; then with the brush spread the paste over the paper, and lay on this another piece; press this down as before and continue the process until twenty or thirty paper coverings have been used. After the first two or three layers, it is not necessary to use pieces which entirely cover the surface ; any sized scraps will do if they are so placed that the same thickness is preserved throughout. The outer surface should be as smooth and even as possible. When this is completed, let it dry for a day or two in any moderately warm place, as it is not well to dry it too quickly. When it seems sufficiently hard, remove the mold, and you will have a pasteboard cup with an uneven edge which must be trimmed with a sharp knife and smoothed with sand-paper.

It might be well to trim off the top before removing the mold, as you would be more certain of getting it even by so doing. After this the cup can be painted in any manner desired.

A plaque can readily be molded upon the inside of a plate or saucer, and a pretty work-basket can be made upon a shallow bowl. Toy boats are made in the same manner as the cup, upon wooden molds cut out for the purpose.

CARD RECEIVERS.—These are generally flat dishes or shallow cups, made to hold visiting-cards, or the varied collections from Christmas, Easter, and New-year's. They may be molded on plates, saucers, or small bowls, or receiving their concave shape from a plaque or saucer, they can be cut into any fantastic form your fancy may dictate. A large, well-shaped grape-leaf, or the catalpa, would furnish pretty designs to those who have no confidence in their own skill in that direction.

UMBRELLA HOLDERS.—Take any cylinder with a smooth surface, about two feet in length, and six to ten inches in diameter, for the mold; make upon it a coating of papier-maché about half an inch in thickness. It is made much stronger by rolling it during the pasting. The bottom may be of the same material, or a wooden disk made to perfectly fit into the cylinder. The whole surface should be thoroughly sand-papered and given two or three good coats of paint. A simple band of gold paint around top and bottom forms a pretty finish, but a large bunch of peonies or poppies, freely painted upon one side, greatly improves its appearance.

By reducing a quantity of paper and paste into a pulp, and allowing that to become a little dried—still moist, but not liquid—a number of objects can be molded, such as animals, boats, marbles, etc., by simply forming them with the hands and allowing them to dry.

Paper pulp is sometimes mixed with common blue clay and glue, instead of flour-paste, used as a *binding* material.

A beautiful vase can easily be made of papier-maché by forming a frame-work of pasteboard, and joining it together with a few stitches or with narrow strips of strong paper pasted across the edges. Make this frame-work as near the form and size of your vase as it is possible for you to get ; then with your thin paper line it inside and

out, until it seems as thick as you desire. Trim and sand-
paper off the upper edge, and cover with one or two extra
layers to insure a rounded edge common in earthenware
vases. Stand it on a smooth, even table or board to make
it flat on the bottom, and let it have plenty of time to
dry. Next make from the paper pulp and fine clay preparation spoken of above a rose, poppy, or other flower,
with its leaves and buds, resembling as nearly as possible
those on the bisque vases so fashionable just now. This
may seem at first a very difficult undertaking, but by
molding one petal at a time, and placing each in position
with glue as it is finished, the work is comparatively simple. Do not undertake a difficult flower at first. If in
summer, you may take any from the garden, and after enlarging every part in the same proportions, make it your
model. When the flowers, stems, and leaves are all in
place, let them become thoroughly dry, then after painting
the body of your vase with shades of blue, red, or olive, so
applied that they give a clouded effect to the whole, color
your flowers as nearly as you can like the natural ones of
the same species, and the stems and leaves the proper
shades of brown or green. Let this paint thoroughly dry,
and then varnish with the white shellac dissolved in alcohol spoken of elsewhere in this book, if a very light surface is to be covered, or with the dark shellac or common
varnish if the surface is intended to be dark. The floral

decorations are not absolutely necessary, and a very pretty vase is made by simply painting the smooth surface with any graceful or pretty design, and varnishing it subsequently to give it the desired polish.

THE JAPANESE PAPER BIRD.

In the skillful management of paper, the Japanese are acknowledged to take the lead, as their balloons and kites, lanterns and fire-screens, now so commonly seen in this country, will testify.

Many of the grotesque and hideous monsters, which

nevertheless are artistic in form and decorative in effect, are made of paper pulp, with the necessary materials added to give it the proper degree of hardness ; and in articles made of folded or crinkled paper they have no equals, while in some instances they apparently infuse life itself into their airy creations. By simply folding a square piece of paper in the manner here described, they produce a bird-like figure, which will move its wings in quite a natural and amusing manner.

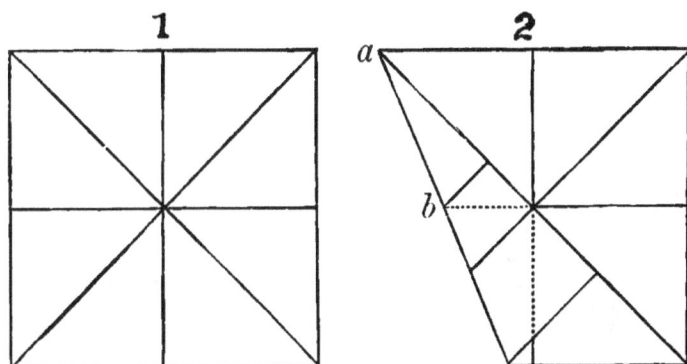

A leaf of paper—letter-paper is good for the purpose—is cut into an exact square; fold this cornerwise, and then through the middle each way, as indicated in Fig. 1. This done, turn over each corner in succession, so that the edge of the square will be along one of the cornerwise folds, as in Fig. 2, and fold sharply the portion from *a* to *b*. Do this eight times, twice with each corner, first turning it one way and then the other, till it has the folds shown in

Fig. 3. Turn inward two of these portions, indicated by the shading, as in Fig. 4; this will draw together the other two sides; fold it closely across the middle, *a b*, as in Fig.

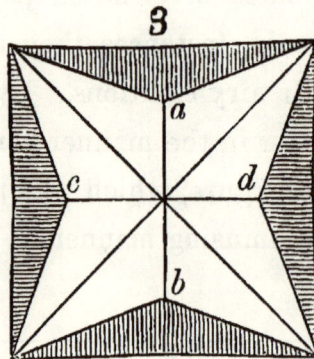

5; then repeat the same in the other direction, folding on the line *c d*. This is done to mark the folds, which may be made more completely by pressing them with the finger-nail. Now it will be easy to bring the corners of the

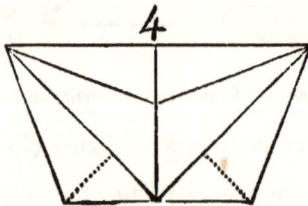

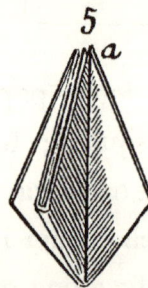

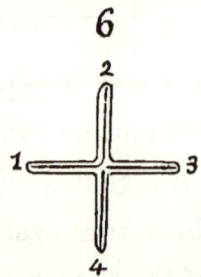

square up together, making a figure like No. 5 or like No. 6, when looking down on the meeting of the points at *a*. Then bring the points 1 and 2 together, also 3 and 4, and your figure will be like No. 7. Take the two outside points at *a* and turn them down, folding at the dotted line, and you have Fig. 8. Now turn down the other two points, 3 and 4, one forward, the other backward, making Fig. 9, with two broad points inside and two narrow ones outside. Turn and fold these narrow points to the right and left, and turn down the end of one point to form the head, and you have the bird, Fig. 10. Take it by the head and tail, as shown in the final view, and move them to and from each other. After a little careful working, when the folds become flex-

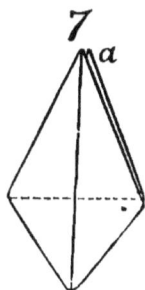

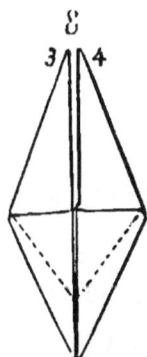

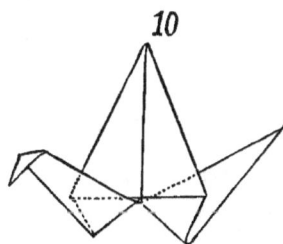

ible in the proper places, you will make the bird flap its wings. It can be done after a few trials, if not on the first, and is sure to afford amusement to all.

THE TUMBLING EGG.

Fill a quill with quicksilver, seal it at both ends with good hard wax; then have an egg boiled, take a tiny piece of shell off the small end, and thrust in the quill with the quicksilver; lay it on the floor, and it will not cease tumbling so long as any heat remains in it; or if you put quicksilver into a small bladder, and then blow it up, upon warming the bladder it will skip about as long as heat remains in it.

THE THREE HALOS.

Take a saturated solution of alum, and, having spread a few drops of it over a plate of glass, it will rapidly crystallize. When this plate is held between the observer and the sun or a lamp-flame, with the eye very close to the smooth side of the glass plate, there will be seen three beautiful halos of light at different distances from the luminous body. The smallest, which is the innermost circle, is the whitest, the second is larger and more colored, with its blue rays extending outward, and the third is very large and highly colored.

PAPER BOATS.

Take a piece of paper measuring about four by three inches ; fold it across the middle, as shown by dotted line

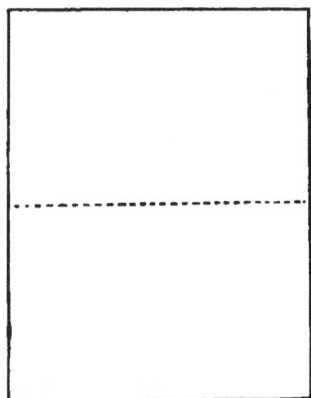

Fig. 1

Fig. 2

in Fig. 1; then turn down the corners of the folded side (*ab*,

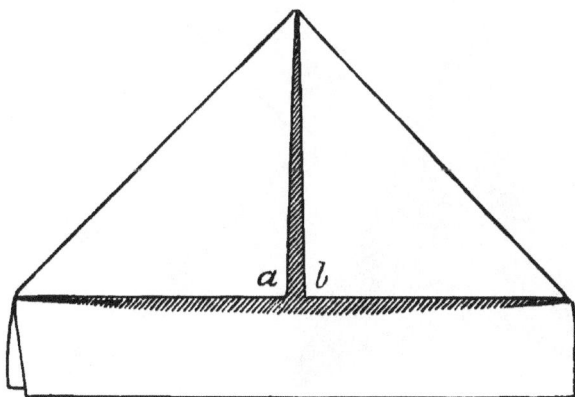

Fig. 3

Fig. 2). You now have Fig. 3 ; turn up the edge *c d* toward

you, and fold it ; turn up the other edge away from you,
and fold it against the other side, which gives you Fig. 4.

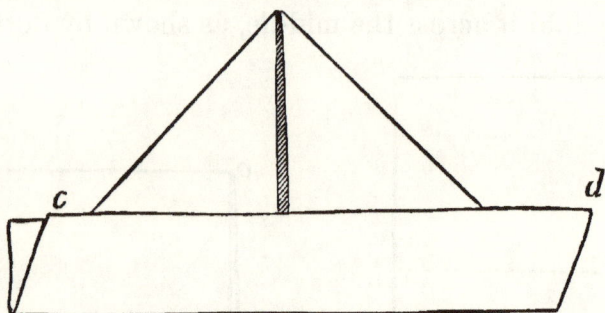

Fig. 4

Bend over the points *c d* in either direction, also the other
two corresponding points, so that the outline of the triangle

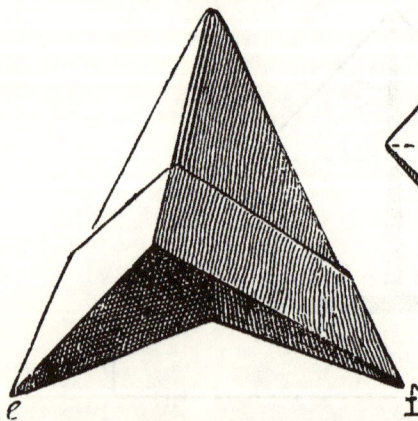

Fig. 5

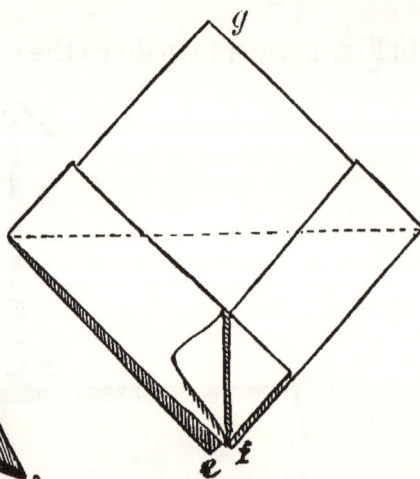

Fig. 6

is continuous.   You can cut off these little corners if you

like ; but the boat is somewhat stronger, however, by letting them remain, and after a little experience, you will
find no difficulty in disposing of them. This little hat-
shaped form you now open (Fig. 5) and press together,

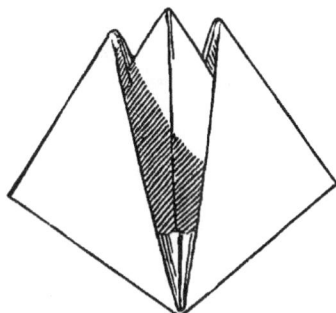

Fig. 7

with the points *e f* meeting each other, which gives you
Fig. 6. Bend the point *f* up toward you till it meets the
point *g*, folding on the dotted line. Turn the point *e*
up likewise on the other side. Now you have another

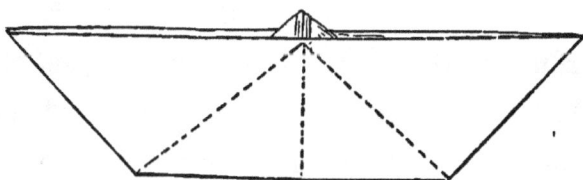

Fig. 8

hat, but smaller, and with a triple crown. Treat this as
before (Figs. 5 and 6). Your last shape will have two
points meeting at the bottom and three at the top. Pull

the two outside points at the top apart sideways (Fig. 7),
and continue this till you have drawn it out to a flat

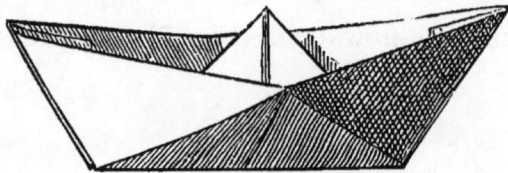

Fig. 9

shape, as in Fig. 8.   Press this closely together, then open
it slightly, and the boat is complete—like Fig. 9.

(NOTE.—To avoid taking up unnecessary space, the first two figures are
drawn smaller than their actual proportion to the rest.)

HOW TO TAKE IMPRESSIONS OF PLANTS.

Take fine paper and oil it well with lard or sweet oil;
let it stand a few moments to soak through, then remove
the superfluous oil with a piece of paper, and hang it in
the air to dry.   When the oil is well dried in, take a
lighted candle and move the paper slowly over it in a
horizontal direction so as to touch the flame, till it is perfectly black.   When you wish to take impressions of
plants, lay your plant carefully on the oiled paper, and a
piece of clean paper over it, and rub it with your finger
equally in all parts for about half a minute; then take

up your plant, being careful not to disturb the order of the leaves, and place it on the paper on which you wish to have the impression ; cover it with a piece of blotting-paper and rub it with your finger for a short time, and you will have an impression equal to a fine engraving. The same piece of black paper will serve to take off a great number of impressions, so that when you have once gone through the process of blacking it, you may make several impressions in a very short time.

It is well for beginners to try with single leaves before attempting whole plants. After you have gained some experience you will find little difficulty in making a beautiful bouquet of leaves, which will be a very acceptable Christmas or birthday gift for mother or an older sister or friend.

A NICE FRAME FOR THE ABOVE.

Procure a strip of board, half an inch thick and three inches wide; take the dimensions of your drawing or impression picture, and subtracting half an inch from both length and width, make the remainder the inner dimensions of your frame. For instance, suppose your picture was twelve inches wide and fourteen inches long, the inner dimensions of your frame would be eleven and one-half by thirteen and one-half inches. The two upright strips would be cut just thirteen and one-half inches long, but the top and bottom would be eleven and one-half inches plus six inches, the width of the two sides, which is seventeen and one-half inches. So the two sides would be thirteen and one-half inches and the top and bottom seventeen and one-half inches each. Great care must be taken to cut the pieces so that their ends will be at exact right angles to their sides. If you are not expert in such work, it would be well to get a carpenter to cut the pieces for you. In selecting your stock for this frame, procure a board with a rough, unplaned surface, if possible, as the result is much better than with a perfectly smooth satin finish. Next take a lath and cut from it two strips three inches longer than the side-pieces, in this instance sixteen and one-half inches, and two other strips one-half inch longer than the inner dimensions of top and bottom, being twelve inches for the frame we are making. With good hot glue join the parts of the frame, and tie it with a cord to keep its form till the glue is dry ; then lay the laths upon the back of the frame, one-fourth of an inch from the inner edge, and with small brads nail them in place. At this stage it is well to have your glass fitted, as it saves marring the frame when finished. After it is fitted—any glazier will do that for you—lay the glass carefully away till needed. Find some prettily shaped larch twigs with their little cones attached, or if they are not to be had, pine twigs will do, and with the hot glue and two or three slender brads, place them in graceful bunches over the points of joining. With a bottle of gold paint and a soft brush you can very soon change this, rough, unpretending affair into a very artistic frame, one of which, if every step of the process of construction has been carefully taken, you may justly be proud. The glass is next put in place, then the picture carefully laid upon that, face downward, and a piece of cardboard—an old paper-box cover will do—cut the exact size of the glass, laid upon both ; these are caught in place by brad-nails driven into the edges of the laths, and extending over the edges of the cardboard. When the picture is firmly fixed in its place, paste a piece of strong brown paper over the whole back of the picture and frame, covering the laths as well. This will exclude all dust and dampness and make the whole thing neater in appearance. Last of all, put in two screw-eyes a little above the middle line of the frame and attach a wire or cord for hanging it in its place upon the wall.

[NOTE.—Before pasting on the brown paper, dampen it well to avoid its wrinkling.]

PAPIER-MACHÉ BOATS.

In a preceding article, I alluded to boats as being good subjects for papier-maché, and remembering how much pleasure every boy takes in constructing a boat, I will give a few more explicit directions for the benefit of those of my readers who have ponds and brooks within easy access of their homes.

Having cut from soft wood a good model for the hull, smear it well over with sweet-oil or lard, and rub it well into the wood; then cut your paper into strips an inch or so wide, and paste them longitudinally around the model from stem to stern, in very much the same manner that the boards are put on a real boat, but not so evenly, as the arrangement will not show when the boat is completed. Continue this process until the coating of paper is as thick as very heavy pasteboard, and let it remain until perfectly dry; then with a sharp knife cut off the edge evenly at the top, and sand-paper the whole surface till it is smooth and hard.

Cover both inside and out with two good coats of oil paint, making sure that every point is protected by this medium from the invasion of the water, which would soon ruin it if allowed to reach the paper surface.

Now cut two supports or braces out of $\frac{3}{4}$-inch board, which will just fit into the body of the boat, across it from side to side. These are to give proper strength and, at the same time, form supports for the masts ; while into a post at the stern two small iron sockets can be driven from the outside through the paper, for holding the rudder in place. The others are placed, one fore and the other aft, in the position the masts are finally to occupy.

As these boats are necessarily very light, some ballast or a keel is indispensable for their sailing well. If a ballast is used, it must be fastened in place by wires on the inside ; but as a keel is most satisfactory in the end, I should strongly advise its use. As it is molded from , lead, you will be obliged to construct your own mold, which can be done by digging out a piece of wood in the proper shape, or, what is easier, by nailing on a flat piece of board two narrow strips at a suitable distance from each other, and closing the form by nailing other and shorter strips across the ends of the first. A little trough, as you will see, will be the result, and if after passing into this your melted lead you place two sharp nails with their heads imbedded in the mass, at the same distance from each other, and in the same relative positions as your wooden supports, your keel will, when hard, require only a few blows with the hammer to fix it in place. Care must be taken to place the nails so that they will enter the supports after passing through the paper bottom ; as the keel would not otherwise hold in place. Next cut from the cigar-box wood a deck for your craft ; this is easiest done by simply laying the model upon the wood bottom upward, and marking around the edge with a sharp-pointed lead-pencil. This deck must necessarily fit in your boat if your lines are followed in the cutting. Mark upon the deck the positions of the supports, and bore holes through it and into them, for the accommodation of the masts, which should be two in number for a schooner, or three for a full-rigged ship ; fasten a bowsprit in its place, and arrange your sails and stays to suit the style of your boat.

After the keel, deck, and bowsprit are in place, it would be well to give her another good coat of paint, and when that is perfectly dry, to varnish her thoroughly with the shellac spoken of before in this book.

This boat is a great improvement on the ordinary dugout hulls most boys are in the habit of making; for aside from taking less time in making, and sailing more rapidly, it has the advantage of being duplicated ; that is, of having a dozen if you wish, made just like it on the same model, while it would be almost impossible to make two alike by the old, laborious method. In forming your model be careful to make it largest at the top, so that it can be removed without trouble from its papier-maché covering.

THE TOY STEAM-BOAT.

Among the many mechanical toys a boy of ordinary ability can make, the steam-boat is perhaps one of the most satisfactory of them all.

As a scroll-saw takes an important part in its making, some knowledge of one, or friendship with the owner of it, is desirable, if not absolutely necessary, for complete success.

This toy is composed principally of five pieces of board, of different degrees of thickness, which are first cut out as follows:

The first piece, or hull, is eighteen inches long by three and one-half inches wide, with a shape like that indicated by Fig. 1, and made of wood seven-eighths of an inch thick.

To insure making both sides of these pieces alike, it would be well to first draw, on thick brown paper, a straight line from the bow to the middle point of the stern, and carefully mark out one-half the piece on the right side of this line ; then, folding the paper on the line, cut through the outline, and the pattern is ready for use on your wood. Do this with all the parts, and you will find less difficulty in putting them together.

The second piece is made of a half-inch board, and is nineteen inches long, by five and one-half inches wide opposite the slits for the wheels.

The dotted line *d e* across this is just nine and one-half inches from the bow, and is placed there to show where the slits *a a* are to begin. These slits are for the wheels, and are four and one-quarter inches long, five-eighths of an inch wide, and three-eighths of an inch from the edge. The sides opposite these slits must be straight, or parallel to a line drawn from bow to middle of stern. The hole in the middle is three inches long by two inches wide, with an extension two inches long by one wide on the forward end. The middle of the main hole forms a line with the middle point of the paddle-wheel slits. Remember and mark out one-half of this on paper, double, and cut both sides at once ; do 3, 4, and 5 the same way.

The third piece is made of seven-eighths-inch wood, four-teen inches long, and corresponds in shape to the second board from the dotted line *b c*, Fig. 2, to just aft of the slits for the paddle-wheels. Here the edge forms a line parallel to that of the second board, but one inch from it all the

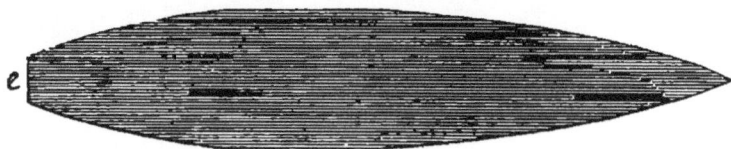

Fig. 1

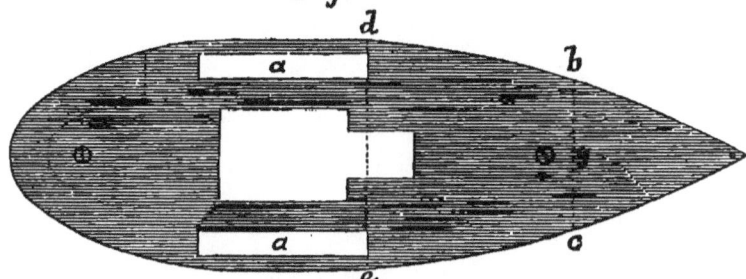

Fig. 2

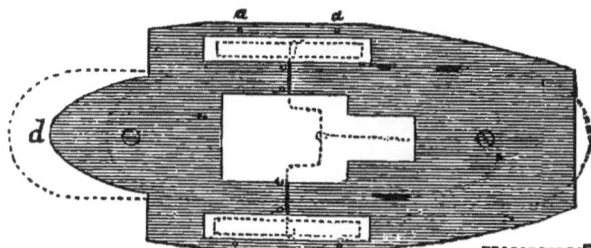

Fig. 3

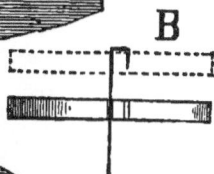

B

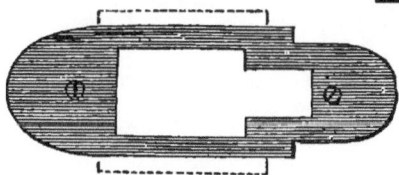

Fig. 4

Fig. 5

distance around, as indicated by the dotted lines on Fig. 2. Its shape is given in Fig. 3, and the point *d* is intended to fall over *e* in Fig. 1. The rear, *f*, in the second board, indicated in Fig. 2, extends an inch beyond, and forms the base for the flag-staff to stand upon, and a hole is made at *g* for another flag-staff to rest in (*see* engraving). The slits and central hole are the same size as in second board, and correspond to them in shape and position. (The position which three occupies in connection with two is indicated on Fig. 2 by the dotted lines.)

Fourth piece : Cut it like Fig. 4 in shape, and out of a board one inch in thickness. Its position is indicated by the inner set of dotted lines on Fig. 3. This piece is ten inches long and two and three-quarter inches wide, with a central hole the same size and shape as in the other pieces. At three-quarters of an inch forward from the slits for paddle-wheels, cut in three-quarters of an inch and finish in a semicircular shape at each end.

The fifth piece is made of half-inch wood, in shape like Fig. 5, and fifteen inches long by two and three-quarter inches wide, with the middle opening corresponding in length to the other three, but only three-quarters of an inch wide. Its position is indicated on Fig. 3 by the outer set of dotted lines. When referring to these pieces hereafter, I will call them Numbers 1, 2, etc., as indicated by the figures.

4

The smoke-stack next claims our attention : this is six inches long, and seven-eighths of an inch in diameter across the top ; its position is indicated at *g* on Fig. 5.

The pilot-house is cylindrical, and cut to correspond in form to that in the illustration. It is one and one-half inches in diameter and two inches high from base line to tip of point on the top.

The walking-beam is rather less than one-quarter of an inch thick, and is two and three-quarter inches long by one and one-quarter inches wide. It should be cut in the shape represented in Fig. 6, and a small hole bored in either end.

The supports for the walking-beam are two in number, made of quarter-inch wood, cut in the shape of *d, e, f,* Fig. 6 ; the base line, *d f,* is one and

Fig. 6

one-half inches, and the height of the support just two inches.

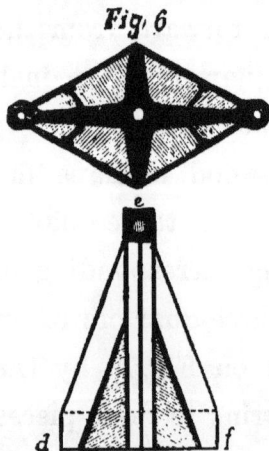

The wheels are made from three-eighths-of-an-inch wood and are circular in form, with a diameter of three and three-quarter inches.

At this stage of the work it would be well to bore in each of these two holes to allow the passage of a good-sized wire ; one hole through the center, and the other a quarter of an inch one side of it.

This is so arranged that the wire can be brought through the center of one wheel and allowed to project a few inches. Then bend the projecting end twice, in such a manner that it may enter the second hole in the wheel when that is pushed back upon it. This arrangement is seen at *B*, Fig. 3, in which the dotted lines show the final position of the wheel.

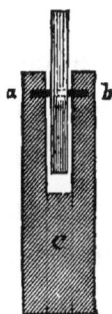

Fig 7

The pieces for the paddle-boxes, four in number, are semicircular, with a base line or diameter of four and one-quarter inches. The form is seen in Fig. 8, which also is intended to assist in the decoration.

Fig. 7 represents a front view of the walking-beam and its supports ; the line *a b* is a short piece of strong wire, which passes through the hole made in the center of the walking-beam, and rests in two holes made in the sides of the supports near the top, and extending nearly, but not quite through to the outer side. This is plainly seen in the figure, the black line indicating the length of these holes. *C* in the same figure is a small piece cut from a quarter-inch wood and intended to hold the supports in place, and to keep them a sufficient distance apart to allow free motion of the walking-beam.

The forward and aft flag-staffs are of large wire, and the two masts are of tough wood nearly as large round as a lead-pencil.

Having all the parts now cut out in the proper form and size, take each piece and bore holes for the screws which hold them together. The position of these is indicated in each figure by the heads of the screws placed at precisely the best points ; these screws should be of different lengths, as those passing through No. 4 require a length of one and one-half to one and three-quarter inches, while those for No. 2 need not be more than an inch in length. In No. 3 make four small holes, indicated by *a* in Fig. 3, for slender screws which are to hold the outer paddle-box pieces in place. In Fig. 3, the lines *b c*, *b c*, indicate grooves, cut down in the sides five-eighths of an inch deep, and reaching across in a straight line from the middle of one slit to the middle of the other; these should be large enough to admit an easy play of the wire which is to form the axle of the wheels. Holes should also be made at *a* and *b*, in Fig. 5, for the wire forming the flag-staffs to pass up through, and for the screws at *c* and *g*, which are to hold the pilot-house and smoke-stack in place.

Having smoothed off all these pieces and sand-papered those parts needing it, we now proceed to the painting, as it is much more convenient to paint each piece separately, and then put them together, than to leave it till the last, as is generally the custom.

No. 1 simply needs a thick coat of white paint.

No. 2 is also painted white. It seems unnecessary to

add that those parts not seen when the steam-boat is put together, need no paint.

No. 3 is first painted white, then the windows are stenciled on in the same manner as given in the directions for making toy cars, in another part of this book. These should be black, while the name should be either dark red or brown.

No. 4 is also white, with windows stenciled on in black, as in No. 3, while No. 5 is painted a buff color, both on the top and under-side.

The smoke-stack is black, while the base is a deep yellow; and the pilot-house is white, with windows stenciled around its sides, while its pagoda-shaped top is a bright, light green.

Fig. 8

In Fig. 8, the two outside pieces of the paddle-box are given; and the manner in which they are to be painted is indicated; these four pieces need be painted only on one side, with a thick coat of white; two of these may now be laid aside, but the other two, after drying, should be decorated with radiating lines of red extending from the central semicircle, to the dark-red line running around the top at a short distance from the edge. These radiating lines should be alternated with light blue ones near the circumference; and the small semicircle at the bottom is a rich dark blue, with a star cut from gilt paper pasted on to give it the desired brilliant effect.

The walking-beam, Fig. 6, should next be treated; this is first covered with a bright green, and when dry marked with black, as indicated in the cut. The supports are first painted buff, the same color as the top, and afterward striped with black, as seen in Fig. 6.

The wheels must not be forgotten, for although showing but slightly, they would give the whole boat an unfinished appearance if left unpainted. These may be dark, or Indian red, with lines of black radiating from the center to the edge.

After all the parts are perfectly dry, fasten No. 2 and No. 1 in position, then having a sufficient length of wire, about the size of a large knitting-needle, fasten it in the first wheel, as indicated at *B*, Fig. 3. Then bend it into a crank, as shown by dotted lines in the middle opening of Fig. 3. This crank should be one and one-half inches wide and three-quarters of an inch deep; make the points, where it bends, as near right angles as possible; then pass the end through the other wheel, and with pliers bend it in place; next fasten the end of the wire, as in the first wheel, taking especial care meanwhile that the wheels are fixed the proper distance apart, and that the center of the crank comes in the middle of the opening.

It is a matter of some difficulty to adjust these wheels, as they should not be crowded against either side of the slit, but turn easily when the boat is drawn over the floor.

After the crank is bent in shape, wind around it the end of a piece of smaller wire about six inches long, as shown in Fig. 3. This wire is to connect the crank to the walking-beam, but it is not to be fastened to the latter until the boat is put together.

The outside of the paddle-boxes should next be attached to No. 3 by the small screws already spoken of, which are to pass up from the under-side through the holes *a a*, *a a*, Fig. 3, into their lower edge. The extremities of these boxes should form a line with the ends of the slits, and the outside of these and the edge of No. 3, which contains the name, should form a continuous flat surface.

The other two sides of these paddle-boxes are to be secured against the sides of No. 4, their bottom line forming a continuation of the bottom of the piece, and their position determined by placing the part on top of No. 3, as indicated in Fig. 3, and making their ends form a straight line with those of the outside pieces and the slits; this is also indicated by the dotted lines on the outside of Fig. 4.

Having fastened No. 3 in its position over No. 2 (see Fig. 2, dotted lines), place the wheels in their slits and let the wires rest in the *bottom* of the grooves; they will then extend a fraction of an inch below the bottom of the boat. This arrangement is intentional, as the toy is intended to be drawn over a floor or carpet, and it is the friction these wheels encounter that moves the walking-beam, and thus gives it the natural appearance of a boat moving through the water. After these wires are pushed to the bottom of the grooves, insert wedges of wood above, deep enough to nearly touch them; make these of tough hard wood, so that there shall be no danger of the wheels riding up out of their proper places.

Place No. 4 in position, first drawing the wire attached to the crank through the opening, and screw it firmly down upon No. 3. There is now no danger of the axle of the wheels getting out of order, if the wedges were firmly fixed, and deep enough to keep the wire in place.

The smoke-stack should now be fastened with a strong and very long screw from the under-side of No. 5, at *g*. It should be very firmly attached in its place, as little children frequently use this as a handle to take the boat from the floor. Fasten on the pilot-house in the same manner at *c*, on Fig. 5. Having the walking-beam and its supports perfectly dry—and it would have been well to have given both a good coating of shellac dissolved in alcohol—take a wire or piece of knitting-needle nine-six-teenths of an inch long, and having fixed one end in the hole made near the top of the support to hold it, pass it through the central hole in the walking-beam, and insert the other end in the second support, then screw the piece marked *c*, in Fig. 7, in its place, which will of course hold the walking-beam firmly fixed. Now glue the supports inside the slit of No. 5, and in such a position that when the walking-beam is extended in a horizontal direction, the hole in the end toward the stern shall be exactly above the line of the axle of the wheels—that is, a line running across the boat from the center of one wheel to that of the other. These supports should also be caught underneath with nails, that there may be no danger of their falling through into the opening in the center.

Having fixed these in place, fasten the loose end of the wire connected with the crank through the small hole in the end of the walking-beam, so that when the crank is in a horizontal position, the walking-beam will also be in the same position. Attach a piece of wire four or five inches long to the other end of the walking-beam, and let the loose end fall through the opening in the top.

Now cover the open spaces at the top of the paddle-boxes with pieces of tin just wide enough to reach their edges, and catch it in place with tacks. Paint them with the light buff used for the deck.

Fasten the two wire flag-staffs to bow and stern, and pass a wooden one seven inches long through *a*, Fig. 5, down into a hole in No. 2, as shown in Fig. 2, at *g*. With fine wire attach a topmast five inches in length to this, allowing them to lap about an inch.

Sink a mast four inches in length into a hole bored through 5 and well into 4, so that its top will be about three inches above the deck, and fasten the stays in their positions, as seen in the cut. On a piece of blue cambric paint white stars, cut it in the shape of a flag, and attach it to the forward pole. A small "one cent flag" will do for the stern, while the name of the boat painted in red or vermilion upon a white ground, should float from the tall staff in front of the pilot-house.

Before the flags are placed, the whole surface of the boat should be washed, if she has become soiled while being put together, and after the flag-staffs and stays are painted and have dried, the whole should be covered with the shellac dissolved in alcohol. Be sure and use white shellac, as the other would stain the white to a light brown and spoil the whole effect.

A hole is bored horizontally through the bow three-quarters of an inch from the extreme end, of sufficient size to admit a piece of large fish-line, the ends of which after it is inserted can be tied together to give a better hold for the hand.

This boat is modeled after the ordinary bay and river excursion boats common to the northern and middle Atlantic sea-coast, but if any boy residing in the West should care to make one resembling those he is accustomed to see, he will find little difficulty in modifying these directions to suit his own particular taste in naval architecture.

THE BOTTLE IMP.

Take one or more small bottles, such as are generally used by homeopathic physicians for their pellets ; cover them with a bit of closely-woven white cloth, and fasten it with a string around the middle.   With oil paint make a grotesque face upon the upper part, and draw stripes or figures to represent a clown's dress upon the lower and

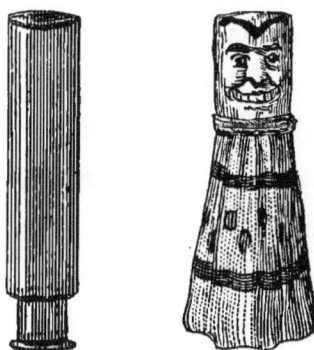

loose portion of the covering of each.   Varnish this with the shellac, dissolved in alcohol, and when perfectly dry they are ready for use. Have a large-mouthed, perfectly clear glass jar nearly filled with water; then, after filling the little bottles about one-third full of the liquid, place the finger over the opening and immerse them, one at a time, bottom upward, into the jar. Be sure and keep the finger over the tiny mouth till they are well under the surface of the water. Should they sink in the jar, you have too much water in them.

The quantity of water they contain should be such that they will barely float, that is, the bottom of the little inverted vials should just touch the surface. This adjusting of the equilibrium is a matter of some delicacy; a single drop will make a difference: but by half-filling the bottle, placing the finger over the mouth, and removing it an instant to allow a drop or two to escape, the proper degree of buoyancy may be attained. Three or four of these bottles, in masquerade, should be introduced into the jar, and if they are, as they doubtless will be, of slightly differing degrees of buoyancy, the amusing effect will be enhanced. Now stretch a piece of thin rubber, such as toy balloons are made of, across the mouth of the jar, and tie it down, as seen in the illustration.

To make the imps dance, one has only to press upon the rubber top, as the air, in the top of the jar, is thus forced downward, the water is driven up into the small bottles, compressing the tiny quantity of air they contain,

and they, in consequence, fall lower in the jar ; but when
the pressure is removed, the air in them expands, and
they instantly rise to their normal position again.

Quite a pleasant evening's entertainment can be derived
from this simple toy. You may first adjust your imps

and make sure they are in good working order ; then prepare a slight introductory speech, in which you can pretend to mesmerize the little images, not letting it be
known they are bottles, and by some wonderful power
you are supposed to possess, can make them obey your

slightest wish.   This will be very simple, as they will naturally descend when you press upon the top.   This pressure should be exerted in such a manner that it is not noticed by the others in the room.   You might stand with your left hand resting upon the top of the jar as if by accident, but in such a manner that you can easily press down upon the rubber with one or more fingers, and while telling of the wonderful things these little fellows can do, you can make graceful gestures with your right hand, and motion with it what you require them to do; it will thus seem that they are obeying the motions of that hand, and will serve to mystify more than ever those of your audience who are unacquainted with the secret.

TELESCOPE WHICH A BOY CAN MAKE.

First, obtain two lenses; the larger having a long and the smaller a short focus.

A powerful telescope, having a large field of vision, requires a lens at least two inches in diameter, with a focus of from two to three feet for the larger glass ; and another lens of from one-half to one inch in diameter, and with a focus of one inch, for the smaller end.   Having your lenses, the next important step is to make your tubes ; this is done by bending a piece of pasteboard a foot long by seven inches wide in the shape of a tube, whose diameter shall be about one-sixteenth of an inch larger than that of your lens. Glue the edges firmly together, and tie a piece of tape around to insure their keeping in place. Make two tubes of this size and one rather smaller, that its ends may fit in the other two. Lap these ends together, and paste or glue them in place (*see* cut). Joining these

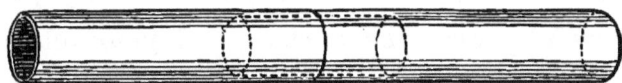

sections together is simply to insure a proper length of tube. If a piece of pasteboard can be found large enough to make a tube three feet long, it will look much neater than the one described above. Take a narrow strip of pasteboard and glue it around the inside of the tube, half an inch from one end ; put the large lens in its place, and press it against the edge of this band. Now take another strip, three-eighths of an inch wide, and paste around the inside between the lens and the end of the tube. By this means the glass is kept in place, it being held by the edges of the pasteboard on either side.

Another and smaller tube, five or six inches in length, and of a size just sufficient to slide easily in the other end of the long tube should now be made. Around the inside of one end paste a band of pasteboard, as in the larger section, but much nearer the edge. When this is dry, paste still another strip inside this one, making a wide edge for the lens to rest against. As this tube is of much greater diameter than the glass, inclose the latter between two disks of cardboard of the same size as the opening in the tube, and each having a round hole cut in its center for the eye to look through. Cover the inner side with paste, and press it against the edges of the strips. Finally, cover the whole thing with some dark-colored paper, pasting it carefully over the surface, and your telescope is completed.

This instrument will present everything in an inverted position, but if the lenses are carefully adjusted, objects at a long distance can be very plainly seen, and a boy can derive a great amount of solid comfort, not only while constructing, but from its subsequent use.

To find the focal distance of a lens, if for any reason the optician does not give it, hold it in the sun, and observe at what distance from itself it makes the smallest point of light. That, if measured, will be its focal distance. The long tube should be from two to three inches shorter than the focal distance of the larger lens.

CHRISTMAS PRESENTS.

"What shall we make for Christmas?" is the cry that arises from the children all over this land and abroad, wherever the Christmas season is known and observed; and many a boy would be glad to contribute his share of labor toward making the others of his household happy, if he only could think of something to make. In the following pages, I purpose to give a few directions for some simple things, which boys of ordinary ability can easily execute.

THE ORNAMENTAL EGG.

Procure a large, perfectly white, hen's egg, and after making a hole slightly larger than a pea in either end, blow the contents into a bowl placed to receive it. Paint some little thing on both sides of the shell—a bunch of forget-me-nots or pansies are very good subjects—or, if well acquainted with the brush, a small landscape, inclosed in an oval, is still prettier. After the painting is perfectly dry, varnish it with a brush filled with "retouching varnish," and, with a long hair-pin, draw a piece of blue or pink ribbon through the holes, and get some lady friend, who can keep the secret, to tie the ends in a pretty bow. A yard of ribbon about an inch wide is required to complete this pretty ornament.

TRINKET-HOLDER.

During your summer journeyings, collect any fine large shells you may see ; the large well-formed quahaug-shells (the common hard-shell clam), or those of the beautiful sea clam, with their wonderful opalescent linings. Scrape off all the outside you can possibly remove ; then sketch on the inside some pleasing marine view, or, if that is beyond your powers, take any simple subject you are confident of doing well, remembering that a very unpretending thing, well painted, is much more pleasing, and indeed ornamental, than the most ornate subject imaginable, if poorly executed or badly drawn.

In painting on egg or sea shell, or, in fact, on any hard substance of a similar nature, use the paint as dry as is consistent with its flowing freely, and allow plenty of time for it to dry. After the painting seems firm and hard, give it a good coat of varnish, taking care to avoid touching all the unpainted surface of the shell. This little trinket-holder is easily made, costs nothing if one has a supply of paints at command, and makes one of the most acceptable presents you can offer to either an older sister or brother, as it is intended to stand on the dressing-table, and hold rings, collar-studs, or sleeve-buttons, when taken off for the night.

AN IDEA FOR BRACKETS.

In making a corner bracket, which, on the whole, is the most satisfactory to make, let one side be as large as the other, with the thickness of the wood in addition, and let the front of the shelf form the arc of a circle. If no curtain or fringe is to be tacked on the shelf to cover the uprights, some simple ornamentation on these is desirable. If a scroll-saw is conveniently at hand, this is easily accomplished. A design should first be drawn upon paper the exact shape and size of the bracket desired. This should then be transferred to the wood and the surplus portions carefully cut away. After the pattern is sawed out, the edges should be rubbed down with sand-paper, or if left very rough, a rasp would reduce this unevenness more readily; the sand-paper should be used in that case, to give the final finish. After the surface is as smooth as it is possible to make it, oil the whole, and when dry put the three parts together with brads and glue. Then oil the entire surface again, and when dry varnish if you like.

ANOTHER BRACKET.

If no scroll-saw is to be had, a pretty pair of uprights are made by gouging a narrow stripe around the entire form, at equal distances from the edge, and painting with gold paint a small stenciled form on the middle of each, also filling the stripe with the same material. For the stencil use a simple one of your own design, made according to directions given in another place in this book. Should you and an older sister desire to unite in making the present, she making the curtain, and you the wood-work, no fancy design would be required. A simple bracket, with well-proportioned supports nicely curving in front, and well sand-papered, oiled, and varnished, would be all required, as the curtain would hide the entire form.

THE CONE AND TWIG BRACKET.

One of the prettiest home-made brackets the writer ever saw was in an old-fashioned country house, in a thinly settled region of Massachusetts. The maker, a quiet, gentlemanly boy of fifteen, was a cripple, and being obliged to remain much of his time within-doors, had utilized these spare moments, and surrounded himself with many beautiful things, made from materials which nature with so lavish a hand bestows upon us all. This poor crippled boy loved the fields and meadows, lakes and woods, with an intensity of feeling utterly inconceivable to his more robust brothers and sisters; but his gentle, kindly manner won their hearts, and the brightest and best the farm afforded, whether fruit or flowers, minerals or young animals, found its way into "Ned's sanctum," as his little room was called. Even the young calves and colts, were brought around to his window, that he might admire their rather doubtful beauty, and nearly every brood of newly-hatched chickens spent several hours of their early life in a basket on the table at his side. One day, the children brought home some beautiful spruce and larch cones, and the little sufferer began, with the true artist's sentiment, to revolve in his mind how he could put them in a form, which should always be in sight from his place by the window. At last he thought of the bracket, and immediately set to work drawing designs for the foundation. When these were quite satisfactory, he asked his brother to saw the different pieces from old cigar-box wood, and nail them together. The bracket was very simple in outline, but the arrangement of the cones, half nut-shells, and tiny twigs, was extremely artistic and pretty. They covered the two supports and the under-side of the shelf, forming little pendants, like stalactites in some hidden cave. These were glued firmly in place and afterward carefully varnished.

THE PEBBLE VASE.

On this bracket was a little vase, made by the same deft fingers. A broken wine-glass held the water, and the vase was formed around this, of that inexhaustible material, papier-maché, studded all over with bits of colored glass and bright pebbles gathered from the sea-shore. From earliest spring till the frost claimed the last lingering blossom, this vase was filled with the fairest flowers of the seasons, and, with the unique little bracket, seemed like a bit of the delightful out-door world transferred to the pleasant corner of the sunny little room.

THE CONE AND TWIG HANGING-BASKET.

The fall after his experiment with the bracket, Ned made a hanging-basket with the same materials, using a wooden bowl for the foundation. This was also a success, but not as uncommon as the bracket. The cocoanut-shell, cut evenly around near one end, forms a good material to build upon. In either this or the bowl, be sure to bore three holes near the top, at equal distances from each other, to attach the chains or strings to the basket. This must be done before the cones are glued in place. If a fourth hole is made near the bottom, and filled with a round-headed peg which can be removed at will, but which forms a part of the design, and receives its share of the final varnishing, the plants growing in the basket will present a much more flourishing condition, as the surplus water can be readily drawn off from their roots.

PAPER BOXES.

Many years ago, when our mothers were little girls and ready-made playthings were not as common as at the present day, during the long winter evenings they were obliged to invent their own amusements, and it was not uncommon in a large family where there were several girls and boys, for them to take turns in providing games for certain evenings in the week. Even the little ones contributed their share to the general amusement, and it was from one of these little girls, now grown to be an old gray-haired lady, that I first learned to make these simple boxes.

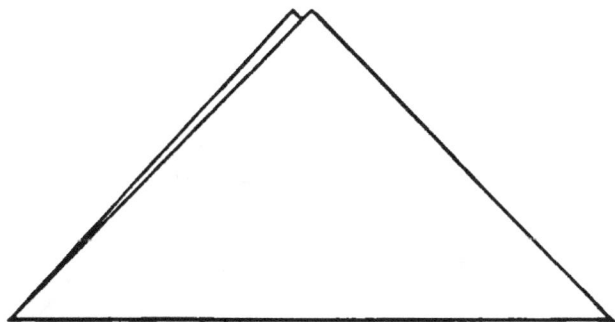

Fig. 1

Take a square of ordinary note-paper, fold it as in Fig. 1, and crease it across ; now open it and bring the two corners to the central point of the crease, and making them just touch each other at that point, and crease

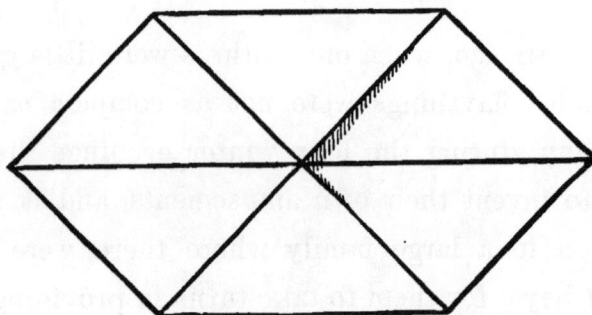

Fig. 2

the folds, as in Fig. 2.　Next fold between these folds
and between the last made, and the corners, as in Fig. 3,

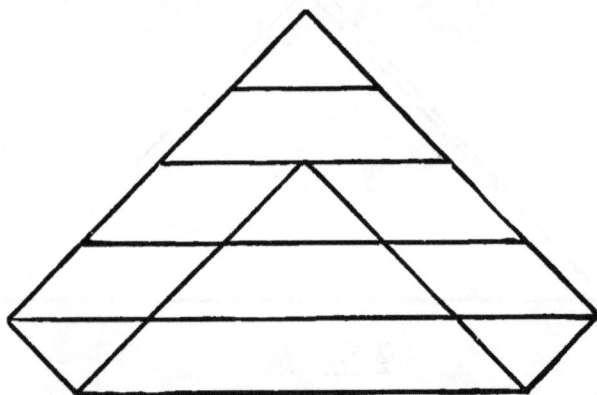

Fig. 3

always remembering to crease the folds when made.　Now

turn the paper and crease it seven times across the other

Fig. 4

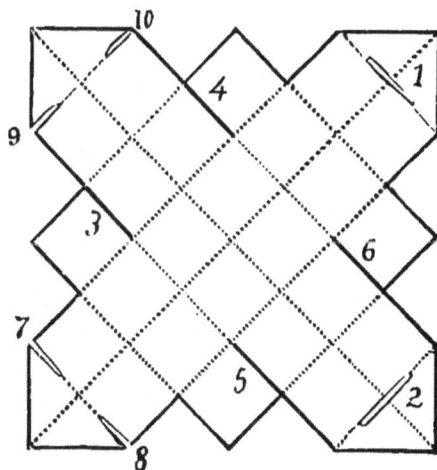

Fig. 5

way, and you will find your paper is folded in little

squares. Then take your scissors and cut the little half
squares left out in Fig. 4. Then with your penknife or
the sharp points of the scissors cut the little slits 1 and
2 ; next, cut 3 and 4, 5 and 6 to the first creases ; last, 7
and 8, 9 and 10 to the dots, but no further. Now fold

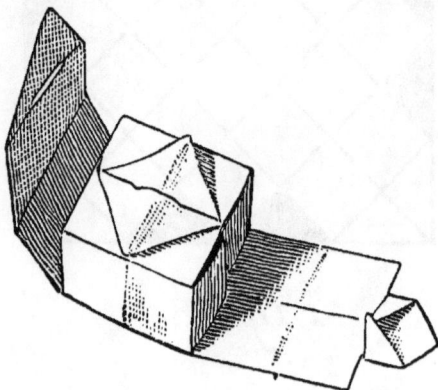

Fig. 6

the joint marked 9, 10, so that it will go through the slit
2, and when you have passed it through, straighten it out
and press the paper in the shape of Fig. 6. Now pass the
last point through the remaining slit and
your box is complete. Occasionally, we
used to make "nests" of these boxes, by
commencing with very tiny ones, and
gradually increasing the size, making one
over another until our paper gave out, or
we became tired of the amusement.

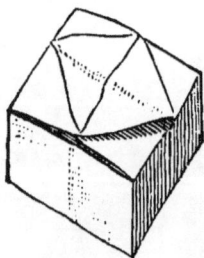

Fig. 7

A SHAVING-CASE.

Although generally considered girls' work, many little boys delight in working upon perforated paper, and they can put this pleasure to good account in making a shaving-case for papa. Procure a piece of silver or gold gilt perforated cardboard, of the coarsest variety, and cut it into two similar pieces, five by seven inches in size. With double zephyr, work an initial or some simple design on one of the pieces only, as the other will form the back of the case. Then get half-a-dozen sheets of different colored tissue-paper, and cut them up into pieces the exact size of the case. When all are fitted, place them between the two covers, and ask some lady in the family to sew them together at the top ; fasten a ribbon of the same color as the worsted to each top corner for a handle, and cover the points of juncture with tiny bows. A little boy in the writer's family made one of these for a dear uncle, and it lasted him a year without replenishing, forming one of the most useful presents he received.

LEATHER WORK.

How many of my young readers have seen the beautiful shoes, boxes, and saddle-cloths, made of leather or velvet, and appliquéd with thinner leather, in graceful traceries, which are occasionally brought over to this country from Russia? These are mostly the work of the women and children of the smaller Russian villages, and in many instances their only means of support.

In those cold, desolate regions, where summer is very short, and the long dreary winter extends over a greater part of their lives, their occupations necessarily must be such as can be carried on in-doors, and are in many instances executed in their own homes. Hence the children seeing the simple processes going on around them, soon learn to help, and long before they have reached the age when American boys begin to think of working, they are earning their own living, and frequently supporting others of the family by their industry.

Although leather work to a Russian boy is anything but play, to a bright American it will be a source of considerable pleasure, and will serve the same purpose of amusement and instruction, for which most of the things in this book are intended.

The materials for leather work are very simple, consisting of the waste scraps from the neighboring book-binders or shoe-makers; these can be chosen without regard to shape or size.

To do the kind of work spoken of above, and known as "Kasan work," select the thinner kid pieces from your leather, and with a lead-pencil mark upon the wrong side any design you may fancy. Then with a pair of sharp-pointed scissors cut out the design, carefully following the lines, and making the edges smooth and even. Lastly, wet the back with a little glue or paste, and stick it upon the cloth. Care should be taken not to move the pattern after it touches the cloth, as the glue might be-smear the material in the open places of the pattern, and thus ruin the effect. After this has partially dried, get your mother or sister to stitch the edges on the machine, and you will have a nice bit of material, suitable for a shoe-bag or any other useful object you may like.

Another kind of leather work which is better adapted for boys, and a much more fascinating process than the above, is called by the French name " Cuir Bouilli "— pronounced "queer bwea" — or boiled leather. The scraps already gathered are suitable for this work, as any kind of leather can be used, although the softer kinds, such as sheep or calf skin, work much more easily. Soak this in hot alum water until it is soft, remembering that thick, tough leather requires a much longer time, as well as a hotter and stronger solution to soften, than the thin-ner pieces you may have. After this leather has been re-duced to mere pulp, press it into any mold you may have at hand, taking care that it is pressed into all the cavities. After it is partially dried, in two or three days, remove the mold, and you have your object in firm hard leather which can be painted or varnished as you like. Many toys for your younger brothers and sisters can be made in this way, and are quite indestructible. Should you chance to have a good-sized piece of skin, much prettier things could be made from it, although a good worker in leather will use his scraps as the boy in his papier-maché uses his bits of paper, pasting them so nicely that no one would guess the number of pieces used. The best paste for this work is made of dextrine, a cheap substance, easily procured at any apothecary's.

A PANEL OF LEATHER WORK.

As this is one of the simplest forms into which leather can be wrought, and one that probably gives the most satisfaction when completed, perhaps the description of a dining room panel, made by the writer's little son, may afford more real assistance to the reader than any general rules which could be given for the work.

He had a sheet of calf-skin, nine by fourteen inches, which he soaked in warm alum water till it was very soft and pliable. Before this, however, he had prepared his foundation, which consisted of a thick piece of pasteboard six by twelve inches. Upon this was nailed or glued a simple design of a duck hanging by its legs, which he had drawn upon a thin slab of wood—a cigar-box cover, I think—and had cut out with a scroll-saw. Before tacking this on, he rounded off the edges of the figure on the right side with his jackknife, and using an old newspaper and a little paste, he built out the body of the bird, molding it with his fingers and an old ivory paper-cutter until he obtained the desired shape. After this had dried he covered his soaked leather with the dextrine paste, and laid it evenly on the form. Beginning at the middle of the panel, he carefully pressed the wet leather upon the figure, using the dull edge of the paper-cutter for the lines and deep places left in the foundation ; always working from the center toward the edge, and taking particular care that each part was firmly attached to the wood. After the bird was done to his satisfaction, he proceeded to stamp over the whole background, using for this purpose an old office-seal which was at hand. In regard to the stamp, any ingenious boy can easily make a good substitute, by taking a piece of hard wood with a flat end, and cutting it across in parallel lines, re-cross these lines with other parallel ones, forming a surface of even diamond-work upon the wood. This, when pressed upon the wet leather, makes a very agreeable background for almost any figure you may like. A wet sponge must be constantly applied to the leather while working, to prevent its drying too rapidly. After the surface was well covered with the stamping, the leather was again rubbed with paste and pressed over the edge of the pasteboard background ; tiny triangular pieces were snipped from the corners to allow of their lying quite flat on the under-side. Finally, the whole thing was firmly glued upon a black-walnut slab bought for that purpose. This panel is the natural color of the leather, but they are frequently stained black, and for that purpose the "ebony black stain" is the best material to use; but it is not necessary that they should be black ; any color can be used, the beautiful bronze powders making very fine effects.

TO TELL THE HOUR OF THE DAY BY THE LEFT HAND.

For the benefit of those boys who make frequent excursions into the woods, or away from the sight and sound of town clocks and bells, I write the following, which I found in an old book published early in the present century :

Extend the left hand in a horizontal position, so that the inside shall be turned toward the sky ; then take a bit of straw or wood, and place it at right angles at the joint, between the thumb and the forefinger. It must be equal in length to the distance from that joint to the end of the forefinger, and must be held upright, as represented

in the figure at *a.* Now turn the bottom of the thumb
toward the sun, the hand being extended till the shadow
of the muscle which is below the thumb terminates at the
line of life, marked *c.* If the wrist or bottom of the hand
be then turned toward the sun, the fingers being kept
equally extended, the shadow of the bit of straw or stick
will indicate the hour.

When the shadow falls on the tip of the forefinger, it
denotes five in the morning, or seven in the evening; at

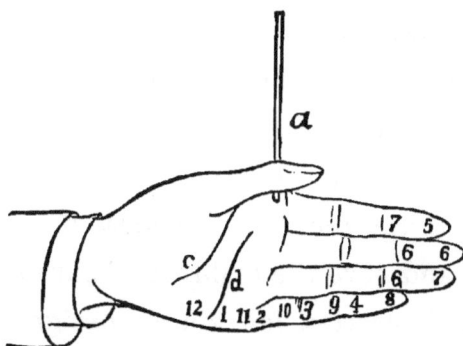

the end of the middle finger, it denotes six in the morning or evening; at the end of the next finger, seven in the
morning, or five in the evening; at the end of the little
finger, eight in the morning, or four in the afternoon. At
the nearest joint of the little finger, nine in the morning,
or three in the afternoon; at the next joint of the little
finger, ten in the morning, or two in the afternoon; at the
root of the little finger, eleven in the morning, or one in

5

the afternoon ; in the last place where the shadow falls, on that line of the hand marked *d*, which is called the table line, it will indicate twelve o'clock at noon.

STENCILS.

A dozen or more years ago I saw an advertisement from a Boston firm, of a package, to be had for the small sum of twenty-five cents, which contained several devices for entertaining children. As the advertisement seemed attractive, I sent for the article, and received by return mail a small box, which certainly contained all one could reasonably expect for the money. Many of the smaller things I have forgotten, but the idea of cutting stencils was so good, and gave the children of our family so much pleasure, that I insert a few simple designs, and give directions for cutting, hoping they may amuse the little ones of other families as agreeably as those of ours.

These designs, which require considerable care in the tracing, should be first drawn upon tracing-paper, or some stiff, thin paper, with a sharp-pointed lead-pencil ; then, this being securely attached to a piece of thin bristol-board, or a common business-card, carefully cut the design, leaving the edges smooth and even. Particular care should be taken to cut all the useless bits of paper

from the pattern. After a little practice, children learn to make designs for themselves, and enjoy it much more than following those given by others. It is, however, necessary that they should use those supplied at first, so as to understand just how the lines are to be cut.

After the design has been carefully cut out, take a smooth piece of white paper, fold it through the middle ; now fold again, bringing the ends of the first crease together; fold once more, making the last crease to fall upon the same line as the other two, and your paper will be in shape like the letter V, Fig. 1. Be sure that *b*, in

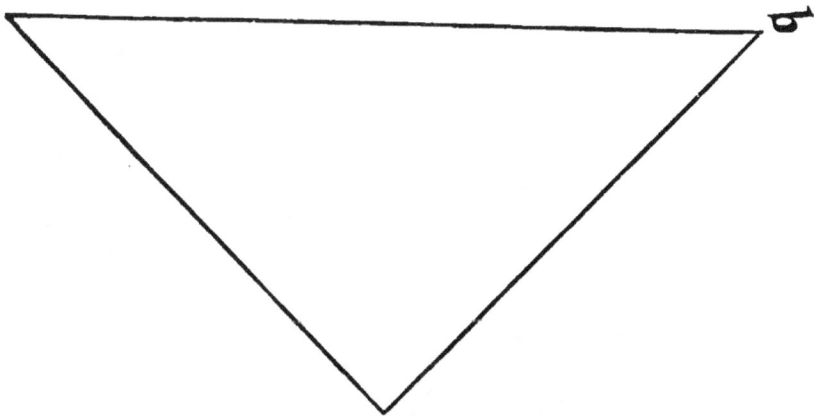

Fig. 1, forms a perfect point. Now lay the pattern on your folded paper, letting *a*, Fig. 2, fall upon *b*, Fig. 1, and taking care that the edges of the pattern fall evenly upon the folds of the paper. Cut the paper out, following the lines of the design. After the black portions

have all been cut away, open your folded form, and
you will have a very pretty stencil, which can be used in
decorating your playthings, or for the various other pur-

poses stencils are so extensively employed. One little
friend of mine used to paste all his finest specimens on

square pieces of black cloth, and after he had a good-
sized collection, he had the pieces sewed together in the

form of a book. On the cover he pasted the word "Stencil" and his initials, all cut from white paper; and it was a never-failing source of pleasure to him to show this

little work, declaring proudly as he did so, "I did it all myself with my own little pair of scissors." These stencils could be cut from variously colored papers and then pasted upon ordinary note; the whole being caught to-

cils could be cut from variously colored papers and then pasted upon ordinary note; the whole being caught to-

gether with a piece of ribbon. A book would be the result, which, if not prettier, would be less cumbersome
than my little friend's, and would probably give full as
much satisfaction, besides being much easier to make. If
you will carefully examine the inside decorations of many
of our fine public buildings, you will see that much of the
work is put on with stencils; and by looking still more
carefully, you can learn just how these stencils are made;

and from them gain ideas for your own designs, which will
aid you very materially in any decoration you may try.
It is not expected that a boy has judgment or skill sufficient to decorate an important room, but if you would like
to try the experiment, you may be able to persuade your
parents to allow you to try your hand at something of
the kind in an unused garret room. But even in this, do
not begin at hap-hazard. Study all the designs you can

find, and note the effect of the colors on each other and upon the color of the wall itself. Choose some simple, open pattern at first, and do not use more than two colors in putting it on the wall. The fresco paint, or kalsomine, comes in a powder, with full directions for using printed on each package. It is put on with a short, thick brush; and is patted on through the stencil. For stenciling, the paint or kalsomine must be mixed much thicker than for

an ordinary wash, and it is best to have your stencil pattern, after it is perfected to your taste, cut from a piece of tin, if a tinman is near at hand. After the walls have received their share of decoration, it would be well to paint the door to match, using some appropriate oblong stencil for the panels, and applying it with oil paint. In such things it is very easy to overload the work, and by putting on too much spoil the effect; so care and judgment must be exercised to know at just what point to stop, as well as to avoid daubiness and an uneven character to your work.

————————

LIGHT PRODUCED BY FRICTION UNDER WATER.

If you should rub two squares of cut-loaf sugar together in a dark room, light would result from the friction; but the effect is produced in a much greater degree by two pieces of silex or quartz; and if two pieces of a fine quality of quartz be forcibly rubbed together, you may distinguish the time of night by a watch; but what is more surprising, the same effect is produced equally strong on rubbing the pieces together under water.

In olden times, before matches were invented, fire for all purposes was produced by means of friction; a piece of flint and one of steel being the substances used, and a tin box of charred linen rags, called tinder, received the sparks which fell from the steel.

Many years ago, when your great-grandmothers were children, in many New England communities a cow's horn, sawed across the top, and fitted with a wooden stopper, was used to hold the tinder, but later, the more stylish and luxurious tinder-box took its place. This box, made of tin, and somewhat larger and deeper than a good-sized blacking-box of to-day was fitted with an inside cover, a simple disk of tin with a ring of wire in the top for a handle, and was filled with a quantity of cotton or linen rags, which were set on fire with a brand from the hearth. When this burning cloth had reached a black color, but before it was reduced to ashes, the inside cover was let down upon it, and the flames were extinguished. After this, another outside cover was put on the box to prevent dampness penetrating, and thus rendering the tinder worthless. To insure further protection against the intruding damp, the box, with its companions of flint and steel, were generally kept in the chimney closet beside the fire-place.

In those primitive days of our country, it was a very common thing for a farmer's wife to run into a neighbor's and borrow some one of these necessary articles, and it was usually the tinder, which she had neglected to prepare when fire was plenty, that was the thing needed. Occasionally, when two or three houses were near together and the inmates on friendly terms with each other, one set would answer the demands of the neighborhood, and would be used by all with equal freeness. Later on, each family made their own matches, by simply dipping bits of wood into melted sulphur, and allowing it to dry on the end. These matches were kept in another tin box, and when the spark had ignited the tinder, the sulphur end was touched to the smoldering fire, and would immediately burst into flame.

Before these matches were invented, however, when the housewife wished to make her fire (stoves were of course unknown), she would seat herself near the fire-place, and, grasping the uncovered horn or box between her knees, would hold her steel in her left hand just above it, and with the flint or quartz in her right, would strike upon the former, till two or three sparks fell upon the charred surface ; the bit of glowing tinder would then be carefully taken from the box, wrapped around with a bit of rag, and blown upon with her breath until the cloth burst into flames.   A candle was quickly lighted from this, to keep the flame till the fire was well under way.

Every boy has probably felt the inconvenience of being without matches, when a fire on the beach in summer, or near the skating-pond in winter, would have been such a luxury.   The next time the emergency occurs, strike a piece of quartz or hard white stone upon the large blade of your jackknife, over any bit of dry cotton or thin paper you may have at hand, as a tinder-box would probably not form part even of the very miscellaneous collection of the average school-boy's pockets.

EXPERIMENT WITH FLOWER-SEEDS.

Split a small twig of the elder-bush lengthwise, and having scooped out the pith, fill each of the compartments with seeds of flowers of different colors, but which blossom about the same time. Surround them with mold, and then tying together the two bits of wood, plant the whole in a pot filled with earth, properly prepared. The stems of the different flowers will thus be so incorporated as to exhibit to the eye only one stem, throwing out branches covered with flowers of different colors, analagous to the seed which produced them. If the plants are somewhat alike in the texture of their stems, and germinate at about the same period, there will be less danger of the strong choking the weak.

HOW TO SKELETONIZE LEAVES.

Among the many desirable subjects for photographic printing, none are more satisfactory or so delicate as a graceful arrangement of skeletonized leaves. It may be very simple, and composed of only three or four leaflets ; or it may be so elaborate as to embrace specimens from trees and weeds, wild flowers and garden shrubs ; while the beautiful seed-pods and grasses, readily found in our fields or along our brooklets, answer for the blossoms in this dainty, fairy-like bouquet.

The methods employed in freeing leaves from their pulpy element, or cellular tissue, as it is more properly called, are very unlike, as practiced by different individuals; but the following, given the author by a lady friend who has a large and extremely beautiful collection of remarkably fine specimens, is very simple, and can be practiced with success by a boy or girl of ten.

Take a wash-bowl, and fill it half full of soft water, into which a heaping teaspoonful of baking soda should be thrown; place this in a sunny window, or one with a southern exposure if possible, and put in your leaves; care must be taken that they are all under water, and not too crowded, although three or four dozen can safely be done at a time. Any leaf which has a firm, well-defined frame-work will make a good specimen. The leaves of the horse-chestnut, maple, silver-leaf catalpa, and magnolia; those of the currant, pear, English ivy, and plum, all make fine skeletons, and many delicate seed-covers, like those of the strawberry-tomato, are very easily treated. Do not confine yourself to this list, however, but try any which resemble these in texture, as a great variety is particularly desirable, if you would have a good collection.

After you have put your leaves to soak in the soda-water, leave them in the sun for three weeks, as that is the shortest time in which any will do. Then look them carefully over, and should any be found nearly free from their tissues, take them out, and wash them off in a bowl of clean water; then with a soft brush liberate any tiny particle that may still adhere to the frame-work, as any blemish of this kind is considered a defect in the specimen.

During this process, be careful to retain the fine thread-like bit of fiber that entirely encircles the leaf and forms an outside frame-work or edge. If it is found impossible to entirely clean the skeleton by aid of the brush, it should be put in a bowl or saucer of clean water and left in the sun for two or three days longer. When they are thoroughly cleaned, place them between the leaves of an old book, and lay them aside until the time for bleaching.

If you live in or near the latitude of New York, the best time to collect and treat your leaves is in June, while they are still fresh and tender, and before the insects have destroyed their shape; but should your home be further south, April or May would be a better time.

After your collection is complete, and all are dry, they will be much improved by bleaching. This process is also very simple, consisting, as it does, of merely dipping them in a weak solution of chloride of lime, and letting them remain there until the proper color is attained; then by slipping a piece of unglazed paper—ribbon paper is best for this purpose—beneath the surface of the water, and bringing it up with the leaf lying flat upon it, the skeleton can easily be taken from the water.

If the form is not inclined to spread out on the paper as it should, take a long slender darning-needle, and with the point carefully arrange it to your satisfaction. Another drying is now necessary, but the bleached leaves should be left on the ribbon paper, which may be put between the leaves of a book as before.

These can be kept for years, and should you be successful and obtain a number of perfect specimens, they will form a very valuable addition to your materials for Christmas gifts, and, prettily arranged, a very acceptable present to any dear friend.

CAMERA OBSCURA.

Camera Obscura, a Latin name, meaning literally a dark chamber, belongs to an instrument invented by Baptista Porta in the sixteenth century.

The principle involved in the simplest and most refined forms is the same, and may be illustrated by the following experiment: Let a small hole be cut in an opaque window-shade, and the room darkened. If, now, the beam of light entering the room by this hole be intercepted by a sheet of white paper, held at a small distance from the hole, an inverted image of objects without will be seen upon the paper. By placing a small convex lens over the hole this image is rendered much more distinct. It will also be found, that at a certain distance from the hole the image attains the sharpest or clearest outline, and that if the paper be removed from this point to any posi-

tion either nearer to the hole or further from it, the image becomes indistinct and confused. At the point of greatest clearness the image is said to be *focused*. Such being the principle of the camera, it is evident that in practice the instrument may assume many forms, provided always that it consists of a darkened box or chamber, having a hole at one end for the insertion of a lens or combination of lenses, and at the other a screen, generally made of ground glass, on which to receive the image. One of the

first home-made cameras I remember seeing was constructed by a boy friend many years ago. In it he used
a lens from an old ship's spy-glass, which still remained
incased in its brass tube. Fig. 1 gives a view of this form
of camera. As every boy is not as fortunate as my friend
in having a brass mounting for his lens, it would be well
to inclose it in a small tube of papier-maché or pasteboard, so that it may be moved in or out of the opening
at will. The box itself was made of cigar-box wood, with
the cover sawed in two parts. After the hole had been
cut at one end and the lens inserted, a piece of looking-
glass was placed obliquely across the lower corner of the
other end of the box, the longer piece of the cover nailed
on the front part of the top, and a piece of ground glass
carefully fitted, with the ground side downward, over the

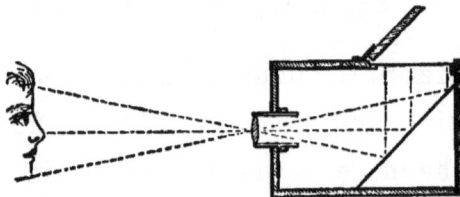

remaining open space; the smaller part of the cover was
then fastened on one side with small pieces of tape.
When not in use, this little cover fell down over the
glass, but when any object was to be viewed the little lid
was lifted into the position in the cut, and served as a

shield to the ground glass beneath. A piece of black cloth thrown over this cover, and allowed to fall over the triangular side-openings, so as to still further prevent outside light from reaching the ground glass, is a great improvement.

In the diagram, the dotted lines show the course of the light from the object in view, through the lens (where the rays cross each other) to the looking-glass, and thence to the ground glass above.

A SIMPLER FORM OF THE CAMERA OBSCURA.

A simpler form of the camera obscura is seen in Fig. 2. Here the case is a small soap or spice box, the lens a con-

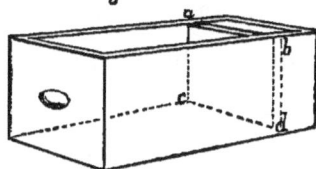

Fig. 2

vex spectacle-glass, and the board marked *b* a partition, serving as a screen upon which the image is thrown. In this form the lens may be fixed in the end of the box if desired, which is much easier than adjusting it in a sliding tube. The focal distance of an ordinary spectacle-glass averages about twelve or fourteen inches, and the box should be, of course, somewhat longer than the focal length of the glass used. A glass from " near-sighted " spectacles will not do, as it is concave instead of convex.

The box is now pointed out of the window, at some well-marked object, such as a sun-lighted building, and the partition-board moved backward and forward, till the point is found at which the image on it is best defined. Then the board may be fastened (as *a*, *b*, *c*, *d*, Fig. 2) and the top put on, of which the end should be cut off about four inches from the screen, as shown in the figure.

A piece of black cloth thrown over the head, and completely covering the ends of the opening, renders the image more distinct.

THE SKETCHING CAMERA.

This form of camera may be also used for sketching from nature, by raising it on end, and providing it with

Fig. 4

an inclined mirror, as shown in Fig. 4. The opening *a*, *b*, *c, d*, should in this case be sufficiently large to admit easy play of the hand in sketching, and also allow an unobstructed view of the image. The mirror may be prepared without much difficulty. Get the glazier to cut for you a piece of looking-glass three or four inches square, and cover the back with a piece of thick paper or card, to prevent scratching; then take a wire of sufficient length, and double it as in *A ;* now bend this double wire in the

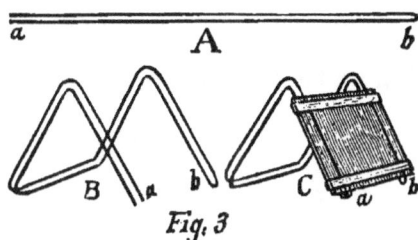

Fig. 3

form of *B*, letting the ends come at *a* and *b*, and placing your mirror, face downward, upon the frame as in *C;* hold it in place by two bands of strong paper, passed around the glass and wires, and pasted strongly on the back, at the top and bottom of the mirror. When in use this frame is placed over the lens, and reflects the image down upon the drawing-paper placed on the screen below. The four round-headed screws in the top are intended for attaching an opaque curtain to the box, which, however, is only needed when the artist is working in the open air. Then the dark curtain is buttoned in place, and falls over the head and shoulders, completely shielding the image from any invading rays of light which might otherwise confuse the draughtsman.

As a matter of fact, in using the sketching camera, it is necessary to turn one's back to the objects sketched, if it is desired to draw them in an upright position. I have represented the artist facing the house, as it would look strangely in the illustration to see him seated with his back to the view; but he is compelled, in consequence, to draw his house, sister, and everything else which is included in the image thrown upon his paper upside down, as a penalty for appearances.

THE DARKENED ROOM.

To those boys living in the country, and having a wide, extended landscape stretched out before their windows, the "darkened room" is a very interesting feature. It simply requires a room which can be made perfectly dark. At the window (if there are more than one) commanding the broadest prospect have a perfectly tight, opaque screen fitted, with a small hole cut in the lower part for the insertion of the lens. Over this fasten a small mirror to receive the image, at such an angle as will throw the reflection down upon a stand placed two or three feet from the window, and thus make it possible for the spectator to view the scene in its normal condition. Should you be desirous of having the whole sweep of the horizon at your command in the darkened room, a simply constructed frame-work is necessary for the accommodation of the movable mirror, and also for the lens ; this would further necessitate the cutting of a larger hole in the curtain. Fig. 5 represents this arrangement; *a* being the

Fig. 5

movable lens, which can be readily taken from its socket if desired ; *b*, the hole in the bottom of the bracket, which should correspond to a larger hole in the shelf *d*, upon which the bracket rests, and can be easily turned in any direction desired. This hole should be large enough to allow the passage of all the diverging rays, and *c*, a small mirror, fitted like the one for the sketching camera just described, to receive the image and reflect it down through *b* upon the stand, or a sheet placed upon the floor for the screen. The height of the shelf *d* from the floor is determined by the focal length of the lens, and must be decided by experiment before the hole is cut in the shade. It is fastened in place by strings attached to small screw-eyes at its corners, and tied upon tacks driven into the window-frame.   The arrangement shown in Fig. 5 can be moved on the shelf, so as to face the lens toward any portion of the view commanded by the window.

PHOTOGRAPHIC PRINTING.

If all boys are not so fortunate as to possess a camera, there is no reason why they should be debarred from all the pleasures of photography ; and as there is much entertainment to be derived from this simple amusement, it is advisable for every boy throughout the land who is old enough to give it a fair trial.   The first thing needed is a frame for holding the print while it is being exposed. This can be made by an ingenious boy, but as it is a rather troublesome job, it is better to buy a small transparent slate for five or ten cents, and discarding the copies, use the frame and glass for your work.   The sensitized paper should next be prepared.   This can be bought at any place where photographers' supplies are to be found ; many boys, however, are too far away from our great cities to have access to such stores, and even those who have will find more delight in making it for themselves. There is a great satisfaction in the feeling of perfect independence, and the more we can do for ourselves without aid or hinderance from the world at large, the nearer we come to the ideal state. So, presuming that every boy has this independent spirit well ingrained in his nature, I will give two formulas for this kind of paper, and leave it to the reader to decide for himself which he will use. The first produces a negative impression ; that is, one in which all the parts that are dark in the copy come out light in the print, and *vice versâ ;* and the second makes a positive print, or one in which all the shadings remain the same as in the original.

FIRST PROCESS.

Paper by this process is very easily prepared as follows : Make two solutions :

> 1st.—Water, 1 ounce.
> Prussiate of potash, 60 grains.

> 2d.—Water, 1 ounce.
> Ammonia citrate of iron, 70 grains.

When these are dissolved, mix them together, and pour them through a piece of filter-paper into a tumbler, and then into a clean glass bottle. If filter-paper cannot be had, nice clean cotton wool answers the purpose nearly as well. This solution should be kept and also used in a dark room. To sensitize the paper, pour out a little of the liquid into a saucer ; then having cut note-paper into rectangular pieces, a trifle smaller than the glass in your frame, take one of these pieces at a time, and place it evenly upon the surface of the liquid ; let it lie in this position until it is flat and not inclined to curl. Now take it out by one corner, and thrusting a pin through this point, drive it lightly into the edge of a shelf in your dark room, and leave it to dry. It is now ready for use ; should any be left after printing, roll it up and place it in a tin box which has a cover, to keep it from the light and dampness. To print on this paper, place your glass in the frame, and next to it any engraving you may fancy, provided it is printed on thin paper and has no type on its back. If a copy is desired precisely like the original, place the engraving face downward on the glass, but if a reverse is wished, that is, one in which all the objects in the original are turned about, and its left side is to correspond to the right in your print, then place it with its face toward you in the frame. When this is adjusted to your satisfaction, take the frame to your dark closet, and put in your sensitized paper, being careful to cover it closely with the back of the frame well fastened in place before bringing it to the light. Place the frame, glass side upward, on a window-ledge, or in any place where it will be exposed to the free rays of the sun, and let it remain until it is printed to the desired depth. It will be noticed that at first the light changes the portions exposed to a bluish color; the operation, however, is not finished at this stage, but must be continued long enough to turn these portions a deep metallic gray. Care must be exercised in examining the print, that the paper is not moved from its position relative to the copy to be printed; with the above frame this will be a very delicate matter, and it is doubtful if it can be successfully done. A better way would be to make one or two prints, without caring for accuracy of form, but simply with a view of obtaining a good color, and time the operation ; this would form a sort of basis from which to work. If some subsequent engraving was upon thicker paper, it would take a somewhat longer time to print it, and if on thinner paper, the time required would be proportionately shorter. It would be a great source of convenience if the back could be cut in two equal parts, and a piece of canton flannel be pasted over both, joining them as they were at first. This with the soft side outward will keep the paper from slipping, and act as a hinge to either half. Now instead of one fastening, two will be required, one on either half of the cover ; if then you wish to examine your print, you have only to open one end of your frame, and carefully lift up the edge of the paper, while the other end, remaining firmly closed, holds the whole thing in place.

After your print has reached the proper degree of color,

take it out and immerse it in clean water, when it will become a rich blue, except those parts which are to remain white. Change the water once or twice, or until every part comes out distinctly ; then take it from the bath and dry between sheets of blotting-paper.

The second way to prepare paper consists in washing good letter-paper with the following solution :

> Bichromate of potash, 10 grains.
> Sulphurate of copper, 20 grains.
> Water, 1 ounce.

Papers prepared with this are of a pale yellow color ; they may be kept any length of time in a tin box, and are always ready for use. For copying engravings, the wings of dragon-flies, or of cicadas, the beautiful skeletonized leaves or delicate ferns, arranged in tiny bouquets on the inner surface of the ground glass, this paper is excellent.

After it has been exposed to the influence of the sunshine, take the frame to your dark closet, and after removing the print, wash it over with a solution of nitrate of silver of moderate strength. As soon as this is done, a very vivid positive picture makes its appearance, and all the "fixing" it requires is well washing in pure water.

The dark closet spoken of above is necessary in all kinds of photography, as light let in upon the sensitized paper would darken the whole surface. To make a "dark room," stop the upper part of the window with any opaque substance, and pin a large sheet of dark orange paper over the lower sash. The yellow paper used in making envelopes is excellent for this, but if it cannot be found, four sheets of tissue-paper, two red and two. yellow, placed over each other, answer the purpose very well.

A friend of the writer utilizes an old disused chicken-house for his dark room, and it answers its purpose capitally, while it was at the window of this little room I first saw the tissue-paper successfully used.

The prints used for copy might be rendered more translucent by rubbing them over with a little linseed oil mixed with turpentine. This, of course, should be thoroughly dried before it is used in connection with the sensitized paper.

A great number of graceful, pretty things can be photographed in this manner; the delicate maiden-hair fern, so common in several parts of our country; the fine, feathery leaves of many of our wild flowers, some of the finer flowers themselves, and many of the beautiful mosses and sea-weeds after they are pressed, make exquisite little photographs, worthy of a place in any collection.

A dozen or more of these prints carefully taken, pressed, and trimmed, would make a pretty Christmas present to a dear friend. The cover could be of plain paper, with the name of the person for whom it was intended neatly written upon the top, an appropriate sentiment on the middle, and the donor's name with the date upon the lower part of the page.

The stencils, for the making of which full directions are given in another part of this book, make very fine subjects for photographs.   If intended for this purpose, however, they should be of a slender, delicate pattern, small in size, and cut with extreme care.   A snow-flake caught upon a black surface, and examined in a cold room, will furnish many suggestions for stencils designed for copy.

THE TOY PANORAMA.

The modern stereopticon has almost entirely superseded the old-fashioned panorama, so popular a quarter of a century ago.

Your parents will probably remember with what delight those itinerant exhibitions were greeted by the young people of those days ; how the very handbills, those wonderful precursors of so many entertaining spectacles, were studied and commented upon, and when the happy day came, how we all rejoiced to see the manager enter the school-house door, and after a few words with the teacher,

address the school, and offer to us children an afternoon
exhibition, for the trifling sum of ten cents apiece, if
enough could be induced to attend.

The panoramas the writer remembers most vividly oc-
curred during the war of the Rebellion, and as the sub-

jects of the paintings were of a very patriotic character,
we had little difficulty in urging our parents to permit us
to go ; and the afternoon session of the school was gladly
sacrificed for so good a cause.

The battle of the *Monitor* and *Merrimac*, was a favorite subject, and, as the vessels moved to and fro, and sent forth from their tiny port-holes volleys of real fire and smoke, while a big drum, out of sight, gave forth the answering boom, the scene was very impressive, and struck a kind of fascinating terror to our childish hearts.

After the many accounts and fine illustrations which subsequent readings have given, at the simple mention of that famous battle, my mind instantly wanders back to the darkened hall, filled with boys and girls, all intently gazing at the sham battle in progress before them; while far back in the rear end of the hall stood the two brass field-pieces, captured from Burgoyne at the battle of Saratoga, nearly a hundred years before, grim and awful, and silently waiting for the time when they should be called to take their place in the mighty conflict then so fiercely raging in our land.*

But finally the war ceased; and after all, the only part the old cannon played was to thunder forth resoundings of joy, which shook our old town to its very foundations, when peace was again restored.

Although children's hearts will never again be gladdened by these great, clumsy shows, there is no reason why the little toy panorama should also be banished from

---

* This building was erected for an armory, but served the purpose of town-hall as well.

among us. The mere delight of making it is sufficient
reason for its existence, and when it is once finished it
will continue to be a source of enjoyment to each little
member of the household in turn.

The simplest form this can have is represented in Fig.
1, the foundation being a small soap-box, the rollers, sec-

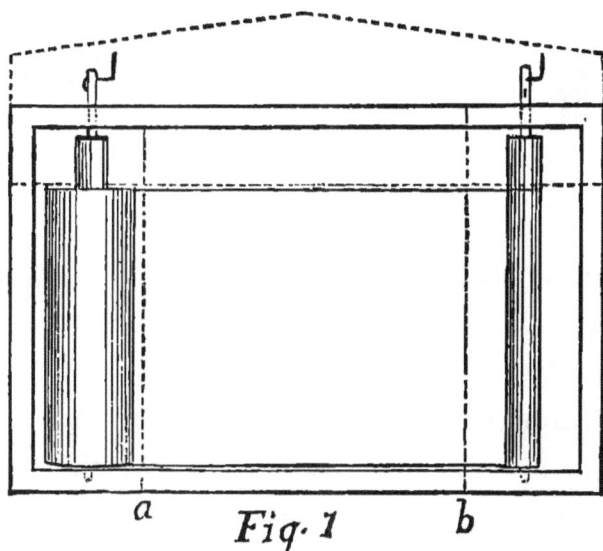

Fig. 1

tions of a broomstick, with small wooden pins glued into
each end, which extend through holes made in the box
for that purpose. The pictures, taken from any illustrated paper, are all cut the same width, about an inch
narrower than the length of the rollers, and pasted together at their ends, the only limit to the length of this
strip being the capacity of the box.

When the paste is dry, attach an end to each roller. It is necessary that the upper peg of each roller be also fitted with a strong crank, as an even motion is requisite for the proper display of the pictures ; and this crank can be made in two ways : first, like Fig. 2, where a piece of

wood is nicely fitted and glued on the pin, or like Fig. 3, which is the better arrangement, where a stiff wire is bent into the shape *a*, and then passed through two holes pierced through the crank-pin as shown at *b ;* this arrangement securing the needful firmness, the projecting ends of the wire are then bent, the upper one upward, the lower downward, so completing the crank.

After the mechanical part of the panorama is finished so that it runs smoothly, two strips of stiff pasteboard can be fastened over the front, corresponding to the dotted lines *a* and *b* in Fig. 1, which will hide the rollers and give a neater appearance to the whole. If liked, a second piece of the pasteboard can be cut, in length corresponding to the width of the box, and wide enough to cover the cranks, and extend down to the top of the pictures.

When exhibiting the pictures, place the box on a table with its front well lighted, turned toward the audience, and turn the pictures slowly, by an even motion of the cranks, pausing slightly at each scene, at the same time giving, if possible, a brief description of the thing illus-trated, as this will add considerably to the enjoyment of the little folks. I forgot to add, in its proper place, that for a final finish the whole thing should be covered with any pretty paper at hand. Nice wall-paper or even com-mon brown wrapping-paper gives it a neat appearance.

A MORE ELABORATE PANORAMA.

Having thoroughly mastered the construction of the simpler form of the panorama, a more elaborate one can be made by simply devoting to it considerably more time and attention; but as this is greatly superior to the other in every respect, it is well worth the extra trouble.

This will necessarily require a much larger box than the one previously described. For convenience in descrip-tion, suppose we have a soap-box two feet long, twelve inches high, and eighteen inches wide. We shall first take away both top and bottom, then standing it upon its side, we have the frame-work of our structure, which is still two feet long, but now eighteen inches high, and twelve inches deep, that is from front to back; next, we

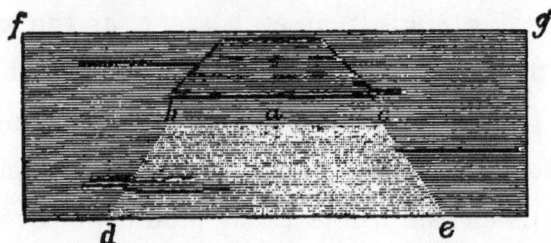

Fig. 2

cut from the discarded top a false bottom, or shelf, like Fig. 2, which, if your box is of seven-eighths inch material, will measure twenty-two and a quarter, by eight inches. Mark the point *a*, four inches from one side of the board, and equidistant from the ends; through this draw the line *b c*, five inches long on each side of *a*, or ten inches in all ; mark at three and one-half inches from the ends of the board the points *d* and *e*, and draw the lines *b d* and *c e ;* then cut out the piece thus marked off.

The holes at the bottom for the rollers are four and one-half inches from the back *f g*, in order to insure that the line of pictures when in motion shall not fall back from the line *b c*, and are equidistant from the ends of the board and the oblique lines *b d* and *c e*, to secure as much room as possible for the roll. Make corresponding holes in the top of the box, taking particular care that they are exactly above those in the shelf, when that is in position. The rollers are made from sections of broom-stick, with holes bored in the ends, and the wooden pins glued firmly in place. Remember that the upper set of pins are to be much longer than the lower to allow for the insertion of the crank. These rollers are about eleven and one-half inches long, and when the glue has thoroughly dried, should be put in place and kept there by inserting the shelf, and fastening it in place by nails driven through the sides as at *i i*, in Fig. 3.

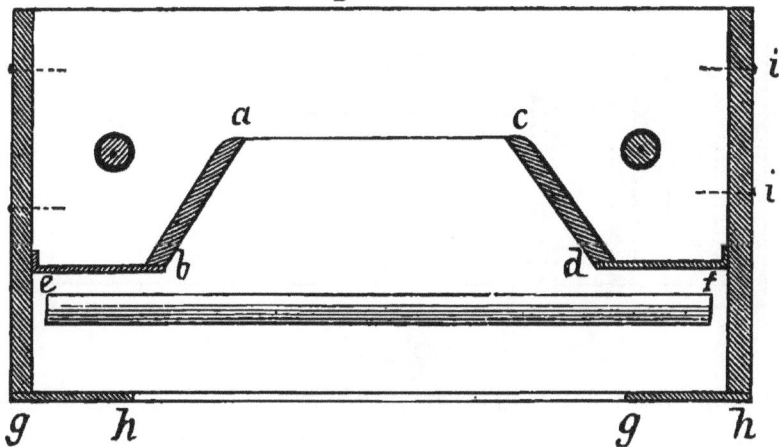

Fig. 3

Fig. 3 represents what is called a horizontal section ; that is, the work is supposed to be cut across from front to back, a little way above the shelf just mentioned, and the observer is supposed to be looking downward at it. Fig. 4 represents the work in an upright position, and the observer sees the front of it.

From the top of the shelf to the lower outside edge of

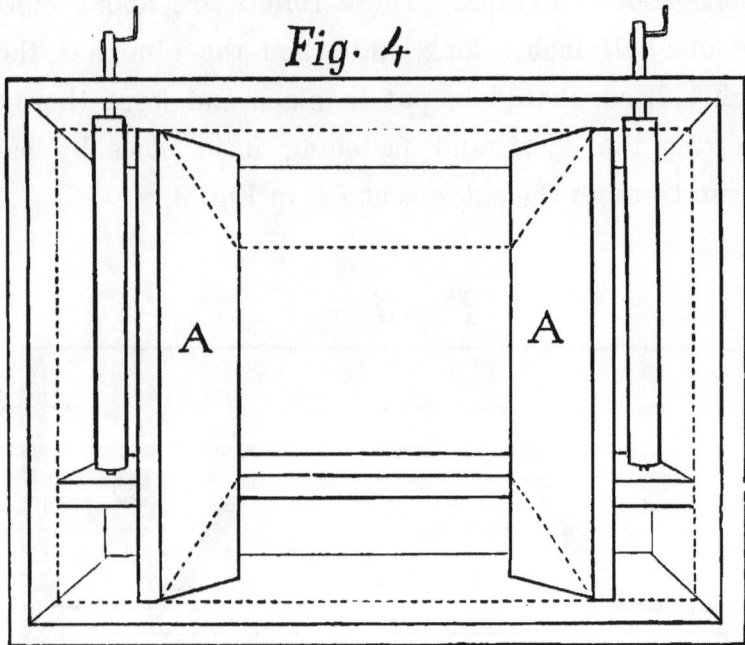

Fig. 4

the box should be just five and one-half inches. Next come the two uprights, *a b*, *c d*, Fig. 3, and *A A*, Fig. 4. They may be made from the bottom of the box, which was taken out, it will be remembered, and let their width correspond to *a b* and *c d*, Fig. 3. Round off the edges at *a* and *c*, and smooth it with sand-paper, as it would soon tear the pictures if left in a rough state; place these two boards in position, and secure them by nails at the top and bottom. Now cut two oblong pieces from stiff cardboard, as long as these wooden uprights, and wide enough to cover the spaces left at *e b* and *d f*, and tack these in position; they are shown by dotted lines in Fig. 4.

From a thin board cut two other strips to cover the spaces *g h*, but leave the placing of these till the work is nearly finished. A board two feet long and about three inches high is also necessary for the lower edge of the front, and should be put on after the other parts are in position, to hide the flame of the foot-lights (consisting of

Fig. 5

a row of short candles) from the spectator. The two pieces like Fig. 5 are made of pasteboard and are designed to furnish the upper and lower portions of the frame for the pictures. Their position is indicated by dotted lines in Fig. 4. As it is somewhat difficult to arrive at the exact proportions of these irregular pieces, without the actual box before one, it will be easier to leave this to the maker, as it is simply necessary to take a stiff piece of paper and place it in the position desired; then crease the lines so that they shall meet the proper points on the uprights; the lower piece comes up to the top of the shelf, and the upper piece comes down just below the top of the picture. After fitting this paper, it is an easy matter to trace the form on the pasteboard, taking care that all the lines are perfectly straight. The curtain should be next adjusted, and a piece of dark blue or green cambric is best suited for this purpose.

Cut (do not tear) from your cloth a piece of the required size, making sure that the sides are at right angles to each other, and prepare another roller from your broomstick twenty-one and one-half inches long. This roller is seen between e and f in Fig. 3. Paste or glue one of the ends of the cloth, which corresponds to the length of the roller, smoothly around it; now letting this roll just touch the floor, draw the other end up evenly, and tack it along the under-side of the top of the box, on a line three inches from the edge. In order that the curtain may roll up smoothly, it is best to mark straight lines with a pencil and ruler, on both roller and box, and adjust its edges carefully to these lines.

Just in front of this line, and at two inches from either

end, tack to the box the ends of two pieces of fish-line, and, carrying the strings down the front of the curtain, bring them under the roller, up on the other side, and through two small holes bored for the purpose in the top of the box, about three and one-half inches from the ends ; next bring the two strings together, and pass them through a screw-eye placed at the middle and back edge of the top to receive them. At one side of the back, in any convenient place, drive a small nail to wind the strings upon when the curtain is up. By simply undoing this, the curtain can at any moment be made to fall. It is also well to tie the two strings together, and fasten a button to them just back of the point where they pass through the screw-eye, when the curtain is down, and they are evenly drawn, as this prevents an extra play of the cord, and obviates entirely the danger of their slipping. Before the curtain is nailed on, it is best to paper the whole beveled surface picture frame with some neat plain paper; very dark red or green "velvet" house-paper being preferable to all others.

After the curtain is in a good working condition, fasten on the two uprights, *g* and *h*, indicated in Fig. 3, and the long piece across the front which you have already prepared ; make a fancy design for the top out of stiff cardboard, taking especial care that it is wide enough to cover the cranks on the top, while at the same time it extends

low enough to cover the upper edges of the curtain and
the rough unfinished wood in front.

Cover the outside and edges of the box with fancy
wall-paper, letting it extend well over on the inside,
wherever there is the slightest danger of that surface being exposed to view ; and lastly, fasten the long strip of
pictures on the rollers, and nothing is wanting but posters and tickets, to insure a first-class show, of the best ap-
proved, old-fashioned style.

REPOUSSÉ WORK FOR BOYS.

The term Repoussé is applied to any sheet-metal in
which a pattern is hammered out or left in relief, by
means of a hammer and common nail, or a regular tool
made for the purpose.   It does not simply refer to brass-
work, but applies equally to work of like character either
on silver or gold.

If you have friends who have made the voyage of the
Nile, you have probably seen the beautiful silver bracelets bought by them of the Nubian workmen as souvenirs
of their Eastern travels.   These bracelets are made, I was
told, by the natives of the interior, with simply a nail and
a stone, but the effect is very artistic and pretty.   So, if
ignorant Nubians can make these beautiful things with
such primitive tools, certainly an intelligent American

lad can do equally good work, with a little instruction and better materials.

This work is chiefly produced by means of a punch and hammer. An ordinary tack-hammer can be used, but that generally in use by most workers is of rather peculiar shape, like that in Fig. 1. ·

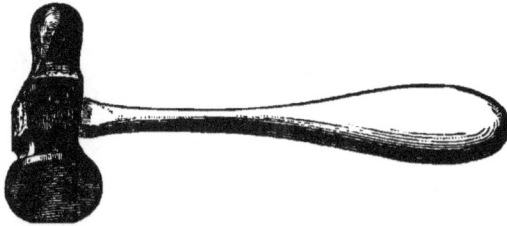

The round end will be found very useful in working from the inside of the pattern, which will be explained hereafter. The punches are of various forms; but a set of common board nails of different sizes, and varying shaped ends, make good tools for beginners. A very nice piece of work can be done with a common French nail whose end has been ground flat.

It is desirable that a beginner should practice upon the thinnest sheet-brass until he becomes perfectly acquainted with the use of his tools. Brass can be obtained for about twenty-five cents a pound, and one-quarter of a pound of No. 25 will be amply sufficient for this practice.

A tool which is of great assistance in all brass work is a dull chisel or screw-driver, with a serrated edge, so that a dotted line is left when it is pressed upon the metal; however, if this is not readily procurable, a common screw-driver will answer the same purpose in most instances. In this practice, the first thing to be done is to draw a line of some design upon the brass with a soft lead-pencil or with impression-paper, taking extreme care that this line is precisely like that in the copy, as all irregularities should be corrected in the drawing, and none left for the punch. It is, indeed, very difficult to make the proper corrections after the work is commenced. Then having traced your line as perfectly as you can do it, lay the brass upon a piece of soft wood, and with the end of the screw-driver pressed evenly upon the line, give the head a light blow with the hammer; then move the blade along the penciled line, so that its edge shall just touch the end of the last indentation, and give it another slight tap with the hammer. If you strike with too much force your line will be unequally deep in some places, and your work will not present as good an appearance when finished. This process should be repeated along the entire design, and a perfect unbroken line should be the result. Until this is accomplished it is best to attempt nothing further. After you have succeeded in making one unbroken even line, mark two parallel lines upon the metal, and do them in the same manner. When these present a satisfactory appearance, trace some very simple design upon the same thin sheet, and after nailing the sheet at each corner to the block, commence with the chisel and mark lightly around the figure. It is often necessary to do this tracing over two or three times during the process of working, as too deep denting at first warps, or, as the regular brass-worker would say, "buckles" your pattern. Now commence at the outside edge of your design, with your nail placed near the line, strike upon it with a light blow, and continue this operation until your whole background is covered with little dents, and presents a thickly mottled appearance. When this is removed from the block, the pattern will seem to stand out from the rest of the surface.

Care must be taken at first not to crack or break holes in the brass, but after a little practice, and a thicker quality of brass is used, you will learn to avoid this danger.

PLAQUE IN HAMMERED BRASS.

When quite confident in the use of your tools, you can proceed to make a card-receiver decorated with an antique head, as in the figure; or by enlarging the design, and making the background circular, a plaque will be the result, which will be useful for holding fruit, or, set in a

velvet frame, will make an ornament for your walls. A
sheet of brass nearly one-eighth of an inch in thickness,
and at least seventeen inches square will be required.

As in work of this character a deeper relief is desirable,
you will find it more agreeable to work over a bed of composition, which is more yielding than wood, and can be made
with but little trouble ; this composition can be obtained
in small cakes at any store where jewelers' tools are for
sale ; but you can easily make it yourself by thoroughly
mixing fine sand, well-sifted wood ashes, or even brick-
dust, with equal parts of pitch or resin ; a tiny bit of tallow improves it considerably. This pitch bed, as it is
called, can be spread on a flat table or board, and the
sheet of brass, after the design has been carefully traced
thereon, fastened down upon it by means of four screws
at the corners. To draw the design for the plaque, with a
strong pair of carpenter's dividers describe a circle whose
diameter shall be sixteen and one-half inches, and within
this draw a second circle, with a diameter of fifteen inches.
The space between these two circles is to be left untouched,
as it will be turned over to inclose the wire which forms
the edge, if for a platter ; or will extend under the edge
of the velvet, if intended to be framed. Be sure and put
your screws outside the large circle, as holes in the body
of the plaque would ruin its effect. In this work heavier
blows with the hammer will be needed ; and a large, well-

shaped nail used for the background. Work around the pattern until it stands out in fine relief.

The brass will become discolored and black during the process of hammering; but, when done, it can be readily cleaned, at first with oxalic acid and rotten-stone, then a final polishing with chamois-skin.

When well polished, take it to a tinsmith and he will make it up for you as a platter, or trim and bend the edges for a plaque.

CARD-RECEIVER.

In making the card-receiver, take the design off on tracing-paper, and then carefully trace it with a sharpened stick or end of a bone crochet-hook, over the impression-leaf on the sheet of brass. In this also the relief should be high, thus rendering it necessary that it should be hammered on the composition-bed. .Polish and finish this in the same manner as the plaque.

FOXING.

Foxing, or sticking the metal to be embossed upon a block covered with pitch, is a favorite method with many workers. The block can be of iron or wood, and should measure eight or nine inches across; this rests upon a deep ring of straw, which is readily made by an ingenious boy, as it simply consists of the twisting several wisps of rye straw in the form of a large cable, and then bend-

ing them into a small ring of even thickness. Catch them
in place with a large darning-needle filled with wrapping-
twine. Nice rings, made of leather, and designed ex-
pressly for this purpose, can be obtained in the trade, but
the home-made ones answer as well for any work a novice
would be competent or even desirous of undertaking.
The top of the block is covered with pitch, which should
be warmed, and then given the slightest possible coating
of oil, whenever a new object is to be placed upon it.
Care must be taken that too much oil is not used, as in
that case it will be impossible to make the surface of the
brass adhere to the bed. In work of a nice nature, where
the lines are many and fine, and the background complicated, this is by far the most satisfactory bed to use, and
when the metal is "annealed" it will be found invaluable.

ANNEALING.

When working in very heavy metal, it is often necessary to soften it somewhat, especially if a deep relief is
desired. This is accomplished by placing the plate upon
a bed of glowing coals, and allowing it to remain there
till it becomes soft, but not in the least melted, and then
removing it with pincers. Hammering upon the cold
metal is inclined to make it brittle, and at times slightly
unmanageable, and this unpleasant quality can be over-

come by annealing; but so much care and patience are required to accomplish this process successfully, that it is not very popular with young workers. In many larger designs, a very high relief is obtained by turning the brass after the plaque has been hammered upon the right side as much as seems necessary, and with the round end of the hammer sending strong, even blows into the figure, at whatever points the highest work is desired. By annealing the metal, and working the pattern from the inside after the background is finished, a very fine bunch of well-rounded grapes is easily formed, and makes a very nice subject for a fruit-dish or dining-room plaque. A dragon, and the emblem of St. Mark, both make unusually fine designs for a mediæval plaque.

As you become more expert in this art you will constantly desire new punches. Designs will suggest themselves to you, and it will be impossible to obtain them ready-made, so it is well for a boy to learn to make his own tools. A kind of square steel wire about one-eighth of an inch thick is made for this purpose, and can be bought in any quantity; this can be cut with a file, and the ends formed into the desired shapes.

A SALVER IN REPOUSSÉ.

A very beautiful salver, which will not only be ornamental but exceedingly useful, can be easily made by one accustomed to work upon sheet-brass. A piece twenty by fifteen inches in size, and about one-eighth of an inch thick, will be required for one of medium size. Strike off with the dividers a quarter circle in each corner, to give it a slightly oval effect, and draw a line around the salver parallel to the intended edge, and one and three-fourths inches from it. The entire central surface can be hammered in the honey-comb pattern, which is so popular just now, and is done with a perfectly straight-edged punch, its length determining the side of the hexagon, or if preferred the pentagon, as both forms are equally attractive ; or it may contain some graceful design done in low relief. The more original the design the more unique the salver, provided it is artistic and in harmony with the object and use for which it is intended.

It would be well for all young workers in brass to examine carefully any work of that nature which comes within their field of view, especially any antique or foreign brasses, with a view toward perfecting their own designs, or gaining ideas for others.

When the work on this salver is completed, take it to the tinman, and tell him how you wish it made up, and he will do it for you for a very small sum.

A SILVER BANGLE FOR A LADY'S BRACELET.

For the past few years there has been an increasing

passion among young girls for the little round bangles, which tinkle so musically with every movement of the slender white wrist, that we are forcibly reminded of the old nursery rhyme :

"With rings on her fingers,
And bells on her toes,
She shall have music
Wherever she goes."

And as it has long been a matter of rivalry, as to who should display the greatest number of these resonant favors, it is quite certain that one of the pretty trifles will make a very acceptable present to any of your sisters or girl friends you may desire to please. They are usually made from ten cent pieces, but occasionally a bit of silver no larger than an old-fashioned three-cent piece is used. The coin is beaten or rolled flat, and the giver's initials or monogram, with perhaps a date, is engraved on one side. Now a much more unique and artistic thing could be made by annealing the coin, and beating its surface flat on some firm, hard bed. After the silver is reduced to the proper size and thinness, with a pen or pencil draw some odd designs, and hammer it in shape with a small, blunt-pointed nail. Ancient coins, such as are frequently on exhibition in store windows, afford excellent subjects for this class of ornaments. When the design is well indented, the work can be cleaned by boiling it in sulphuric acid and water, and polishing it with chamois-skin.

A BANGLE BRACELET.

A bangle bracelet can be easily made of hammered work, from a narrow strip of sheet-silver, which can be obtained from any silversmith at a small cost. The de-sign is to be traced on the silver in the same manner as upon the sheet-brass, and great care must be taken in the working out of each little detail. When the work is fin-ished, it should be sent to a jeweler to be made up and polished. This is of course an expensive, as well as a very nice piece of work, and should not be tried until considerable skill in the manipulation of sheet-metal has been acquired, and success seems in a large degree certain.

Many ladies are fine workers in repoussé, and it cannot fail to be a source of satisfaction to every one interested in the art to know, that each year its merits are becoming more fully known and appreciated by that great class of people, whose purchases govern the prices of all artistic things. Now, boys, I have simply touched upon this very interesting subject of repoussé, and given you a few directions, culled from my own experience. If, however, I have succeeded in stimulating in you a desire to pursue this subject further, you will find many excellent helps, in the form of books or pamphlets, in any of our large stores devoted to artists' materials and supplies.

A FRAME FOR A PLAQUE.

A fine frame for any kind of plaque, whether repoussé, porcelain, leather work, or papier-maché, can be easily made from a square piece of wood, about six inches wider than the subject to be framed ; this can be beveled at the edges, or left as when sawed. In the center, with a strong pair of carpenter's dividers describe a circle, whose diameter shall be half an inch shorter than that of the plaque. Bevel the front edge of this opening, then covering the whole front surface of this wood with thin glue, lay it, face downward upon the piece of plush or velvet, intended to cover it ; the material lying flat and smooth, with its raised surface downward, upon an uncovered table. Cut the center of the cloth away, allowing enough on the edge to draw over the opening of the frame ; slash this to within a short distance of the wood, that it may lay evenly when finished ; now glue this firmly down upon the back, and bring over the outside edges and fix them in the same way. When this is dry, fasten in your plaque with brads driven into the back of the frame, and extending over the edge of the opening at its back. Finally, when certain all is securely fastened, wet a piece of brown paper, cut to exactly cover the entire back of plaque and frame both, cover it with paste and press it in place. It is necessary to wet the paper first, to prevent its wrinkling or forming great bubbles when dry. When the paper is dampened, a bit of paste around the edge is all that is necessary to hold it in place.

After this backing is completed, a couple of screw-eyes and a wire cord are to be added, and your plaque is ready for your walls.

THE AQUARIUM.

The name aquarium was formerly sometimes given to a tank or cistern placed in a hot-house, and intended for the cultivation of aquatic plants ; but in later years its signification has widened, so that it now embraces animals as well as plants in its category. Its use seems to have been known nearly a hundred years ago, and a number of gentlemen, in the latter part of the eighteenth century, made several successful experiments by means of this "scientific plaything," as some writer has happily called it. The aquarium can be used for either salt or fresh water animals, the former necessitating a residence conveniently near the sea, for the purpose of occasionally

replenishing it with a fresh supply of the water. It may be an ordinary globe, or it can be made of slabs of heavy glass, fastened inside an iron frame-work, with a peculiar kind of cement, made specially for the purpose. They can be obtained in different sizes at several places in New York and other cities, and as the materials in themselves are expensive, and the work of making one usually results in a series of disappointments, and finally, in total failure, the expediency of buying one ready-made cannot be too strongly urged upon the young naturalist. Although the large aquarium accommodates more inmates, the globe is much more easily cleaned, and answers equally well for a few fishes, as the one in my window will testify. As fresh-water animals and plants are more accessible to the larger proportion of boys in the country, and the globe much cheaper, while it occupies less space than the large square articles alluded to above, it may possibly not come amiss for me to give, for the benefit of those of my readers who are interested in the subject, a description of my own fresh-water aquarium, and what little experience I have derived from it.

It is a globe of ordinary shape, and has the capacity of a common water-pail. For several years it was stocked with gold-fish, but it was, moreover, a source of ceaseless anxiety and trouble. The fish would die or turn black without any apparent cause, and, still worse, would frequently have what we termed "fits" in the night, and jump out of the globe on the floor, where they would be found, cold and lifeless, in the morning.

The experiment of keeping these decidedly troublesome pets was finally given up, and the empty globe placed high and dry upon a closet shelf.

One day nearly a year ago, a young member of our household brought home three small fishes (the common dace), and begged so hard that the globe might be brought out, and converted into the family fish-pond once more, that we finally consented, and the little fishes were soon at home in our library window. Not more than a week after this, a genuine mud-turtle was added to the collection, and, strange as it may seem, these little creatures have lived at peace with each other ever since.

We covered the bottom with a few pebbles from the brook, and afterward added some sand and a handful of shells from the sea-shore.

We experimented with several species of water-plants, but were convinced that a tiny fine-leaved plant, of which I have forgotten the name, but which grows very plentifully in our northern fresh-water brooklets, and the *vallisneria Spiralis*, or common 'tape or eel-grass, gave the greatest satisfaction on the whole. With these little plants growing on its bottom, we are not obliged to change the water for several days at a time.

In bright sunny weather the plants give forth plenty of oxygen for the fishes to breathe. This can be readily seen by noting the little air-bubbles adhering to the leaves and stems, or rising slowly to the surface of the water; but in cloudy weather this gas-making process diminishes, so that after awhile the air becomes vitiated, and the fishes, finding it hard to breathe, are forced to swim near the top, with their heads at the surface of the water. At such times it is well to introduce fresh air into the water, by filling a cup with the water, and, holding it an inch or two above the surface, pour it slowly back into the globe; by repeating this process several times the water is made comparatively pure once more. Another and easier way of accomplishing this is by using a small syringe instead of the cup; but care must be taken in either case to avoid hitting the fish with the descending stream.

Their food consists of angle-worms and flies in summer, and bits of fresh meat cut very fine with the scissors, during the colder portions of the year.

THE SALT-WATER AQUARIUM.

The globe answers equally as well for salt as for fresh water fish, provided its inmates are not crowded and are supplied with a sufficient quantity of good sea-water. In obtaining this supply, it is desirable to have it dipped from deep water some distance from the shore, or from the channel if possible.

In preparing your globe, put a handful of gravel and sand on the bottom, then with three or four irregular stones build a cave or little arch, for the fishes to play beneath.

Although some authorities say that the aquarium should be kept in the shade, the one with which the writer was familiar through childhood always stood in a south window, which was only partially shaded by some great trees in the garden beyond.

Occasionally, on very sunny days in spring or early summer, before the leaves were fully grown, a newspaper would be placed between the glass and the window-pane, or over a corner of the top, to give the desired protection; but the tiny cavern usually supplied sufficient shade, and it was ever a source of unabating amusement to watch the little fellows swim in and out through the arches, darting now here and again there, hiding in the shadow of some moss-grown stone, to spring out a moment later upon an unsuspecting companion swimming leisurely by ; their little games of hide-and-seek and of tag were very entertaining to witness, and we children would frequently find ourselves quite excited over the success or failure of our special favorite in the game.

As the aquarium of which I speak was a large one, it frequently had several inmates at the same time ; among these the little nippers, or, as the dwellers along the coast of New York State call them, killie-fish—so named by the Dutch settlers from their frequenting the little kills, or inlets, along the shore—always held a conspicuous place. Indeed, these little fishes seem to be blessed with a long string of names entirely disproportionate to the size of their tiny little bodies. In some places they are known as minnows, while on the shores of the Narragansett they retain their old Indian name of Mummychog. They are a bright, lively little fish, darting through the water with such rapidity, that you hold your breath in fear lest they dash themselves against the glass at the end, but they never do ; just as contact with it seems a matter of certainty, they suddenly turn a sharp angle, face about, and perhaps come to the front and peer at you through the glass, with their funny little faces pressed up close to its surface. They are of a greenish-gray color upon the back, which gradually shades to a bright silvery tone at the sides, and their eyes, which are large and staring, have a very mild, good-natured expression.

Very different from these are the sticklebacks (*Gasterosteus*), also fine subjects for the aquarium, for a more pugnacious or plucky little fellows it would be hard to find than these graceful little tyrants, which in early

spring are found in our creeks and salt-water ditches in
great abundance. As this is the only season of the year
in which they can be captured, it is best to be on the
watch for them during the last of March or the first of
April. A dip-net, made of a piece of mosquito netting
caught over a small hoop, and attached to a long, slender
handle, is best for catching all kinds of fish for the aquarium, and the shores of bays or salt-water streams supply
a greater abundance than the open sea, or the shore
washed by the heavy ocean waves. If your globe is the
vessel you are to use, the sticklebacks will afford you
quite as much amusement as any fish you could find, for
aside from their quick, lively manner, they are a very
handsome fish. The male is of a rich ruddy color, his
little silvery sides giving forth gleams of red or blue,
which vary considerably, according to his temper. If he
feels quiet and peaceful, they are pale and soft in tone,
but if indignant, they become very brilliant, and the little
chap with his savage, fiery eye, becomes an object of
great respect and terror to all the other denizens of the
water within reach of his teeth or sharp little spines.
The female is less brilliantly colored than the male, is
blunter in build, and has a comparatively mild disposition,
leaving all little differences with other fish for her liege
lord and master to settle, for which duty he is perfectly
well fitted and takes great delight in performing ; indeed,

so quarrelsome were these little fellows, that they would soon kill all fish of other species in the tank, and when no other subject was at hand, would fall to and fight one another, biting as ugly dogs might do, and spearing with their tiny spines, till one had acquired complete supremacy over all the rest. It is very interesting to watch the process of their nest-building, and to see them, like so many lilliputian carpenters, lay the sticks and hairs in place, working as if their whole life depended upon their unceasing exertions. We used to put in bits of broom-corn split in threads, and bristles from the floor-brush, for materials; and the work of building would generally occupy three or four days. The nest was built in one corner of the box (we were obliged to keep the stickle-backs in a separate glass case, as they killed all the other fish if together) and well up on the sides, with a tiny round hole at the top for the fish to go in and out. After a short time—I do not remember now just how long—hundreds of little fish came out from the nest, and were very lively for two or three days, but in a week they were all dead, and the parents had the waters to themselves once more. We never succeeded in raising the young fish, I remember, but I do not now recall whether any reason was ever ascribed to our failure, or if it was even known.

But to go back to our large aquarium. Fortunately for us, not many fish are as quarrelsome as the stickle-

backs, and most of those I shall now describe live together in perfect harmony. The young of larger fish do
very nicely for a time in the aquarium, and a young eel is
a rather amusing although somewhat sluggish fellow to
keep.

The most amusing denizens are creatures of the crab
family. The little hermit-crabs, found in quantities on
any shelving beach of the bay or sea inlet, create much
sport for the young naturalist. These little crabs, you
must know, are soft little fellows, for whom nature in a
frugal moment prepared no house or covering to protect
them from the thumps they might receive from both
water and stones ; but the little fellows, with a shrewdness
one would hardly suspect in creatures so small, rise equal
to the occasion, and help themselves to the empty snail-
shells left by their more fortunate neighbors. When
small they occupy the little black snail-shells, moving
from a smaller to a larger as they increase in size. After
outgrowing these plainer homes they take possession of
the pretty grayish-white shells also found in abundance
on our shores. It is frequently quite amusing to watch
two fight over a particularly desirable one, which either
has chosen for its own, and ofttimes the battle will be
long and heavy before either will give up that which he
considers by rights his own. If you have one or more of
these little wanderers in your globe, remember to put in

two or three empty snail-shells for them to flee to when
they have outgrown their present abode. Their manner
of eating affords a very entertaining spectacle. Clams,
either soft or hard, cut into tiny bits, form the principal
food for all the dwellers in the aquarium, and a long stick
with a needle driven in one end, to form a tiny spear, is
used in passing it to them. When a particular crab is to
be fed, a bit of clam is taken up on the needle, and lowered down in the water to a position directly in front of
him. At first, before he has become acquainted with this
mode of dining, he draws in his claws, and nothing but
the shell is to be seen upon the bottom ; but in a few moments the little fellow lets himself out again, little by
little, with a quick, jerky movement, till at last his two
little eyes stand in an upright position, and he is ready to
seize the tempting morsel. This he does with his longest
claw, and holding the clam firm in his grasp, he proceeds
to pick it in pieces with the other long claw, and pass it
along to the smaller set, which in turn give it to the next
in order, until it finally disappears in the mouth itself,
and is swallowed by the little creature.

It is important to have two or three snails in your globe
to act as scavengers, and keep the water free from the
refuse which would otherwise remain on the bottom.
These little creatures are often seen moving slowly along
on the surface of the glass, feeding upon the green moss

or confervæ which accumulates so quickly on all the objects under water. The pipe-fish, a peculiarly shaped specimen, comparatively rare on our Atlantic coast, is worthy a place in your collection; and the shrimp, the acrobat of the aquarium, whose funny little backward movements, when the poor little fellow is frightened, create so much laughter among the little folks, must not be forgotten. Young scallops are very pretty, and when left undisturbed open their shells a trifle, disclosing a beautiful fringe of tiny blue tentacles which wave to and fro with every motion of the water.

The medusæ, also called jelly-fish, with their umbrella-like cover, and long, slender tentacles streaming downward, are pretty for a time, but do not live long after they are taken from the sea. The Cydippe and the Beroe are very lovely specimens of this class, the former particularly is noticeable for its beautiful iridescent colors. The beautiful orange colored medusa is an unsafe inmate, as he very soon kills all the fishes within his reach.

If it is possible, obtain one or more of the beautiful sea-anemones, and add it to your globe; the large, bright-colored members of this class are only to be found in the tropics, but very pretty, delicate specimens are sometimes found in our northern waters, where a rock or bit of stone-work is constantly washed over by a swift current. If possible, it is better to take the stone on which they rest, as it

is almost impossible to remove them from its surface without killing them. This was, however, done several times with success, and the anemones lived in our aquarium as long as they could be expected to exist in perfectly quiet water. When these creatures are at rest or frightened they draw down into little shapeless masses; but when looking for food they stretch up again, and expand on the top of the long stalk, as we may call it, a beautiful flower-like head, resembling an aster in form, and of a deep brownish-yellow color. When food is passed down to this animated blossom, it will fold its little tentacles one by one around it, and pass it down into its mouth, open to receive it, but which is entirely hidden by the beautiful petals of this delicate flower.

All of you have probably noticed the serpulæ, or worm-like excrescences often seen upon oyster and other hard shells. If one of these shells be taken from the water and immediately placed on the bottom of your aquarium, after a few days, when the little animals feel quite at home, they send out of one end of their slender tubes bunches of the loveliest, delicate brown fern-like feelers, which sway about in the water like the beautiful roadside ferns in a gentle summer breeze.

But in the salt as in the fresh water aquarium, vegetation is necessary for a healthful condition of the inmates. Here we see on a miniature scale that wonderful balance of organic forces which exists on the larger globe around us. The vegetation exhales the purifying oxygen, which renders the water fit for sustaining animal life ; the fishes and other animals in their turn give forth the carbonic-acid gas, which is equally needed for the healthful development of the plants ; while, last of all, the snails—those little scavengers nature has so wisely provided—remove such minute portions of decaying matter as might otherwise pass unnoticed, and so contaminate the entire water in the globe.

THE WOODEN WINDMILL.

So common were these little toys among the companions of my childhood, that it seemed almost superfluous to insert what I supposed every boy must be familiar with ; but upon questioning my young friends, I find that very few of them away from the sea-coast towns of New England, and the sailor-like influence or atmosphere which permeates them, know anything of the pretty little windmills, or weather-vanes, which we copied from those of our sailor friends.

It was no uncommon thing in those days for some boy less ingenious than his companions to use a little strategy, and so get his work done for him by proxy ; and the

manner in which he would proceed was generally something like this : Early some bright spring morning, with
jackknife and shingle in hand, he would saunter down to
the wharf, upon which he knew at an early hour the old
sea captains of the village would assemble, and wait his
chance. Here the old captains, and the sailors, who by
reason of their advanced age took the same honorary
title, were wont to gather on the sunny side of the
weather-beaten old store-house, and watch from under
their heavy gray eyebrows the bay stretched out before
them, while they enjoyed their pipes, and lived over
again the wonderful adventures and disasters of their
successive voyages ; and here he would watch for his
prey, little suspected by those kindly old souls, who had,
years long gone by, ruled with iron will over the crews
and destinies of great ships, known to him only by their
names. Occasionally two or three would arrive at the
wharf together, and he knew his chances were gone for
that day at least ; but usually some one, whose breakfast
may not have claimed as much attention as usual, would
be seen making his way down the quiet village street,
easily recognized by his rolling gait, his inseparable pipe,
and manner of scanning the clouds and horizon. Now
our friend would begin to whittle in earnest, soon attract-
ing the attention of the ancient mariner by his awkward
movements. Of course, he would receive no end of ridi-

cule for his stupidity ; but as that did not sink very deep
in his boyish soul, he was prepared to pay a greater price,
if necessary, for the work he expected to receive. It not
unfreqently happened that the old fellow would take the
shingle to show him how to begin, and would get so much
interested in the work that he would offer to do it during
the day, and would actually whittle away on the little
boat, while he or one of his companions related for the
fiftieth time how the *Nautilus* passed through so many
hair-breadth escapes, and finally reached port at last,
with no soul missing and cargo untouched.

It was during these long voyages, when time hung
heavily on their hands, that they acquired their skill in
fashioning these mechanical toys, which almost always
had for their motive power the wind or the waves.

The simplest form of windmill from this source I remember seeing is very easily constructed. It is made

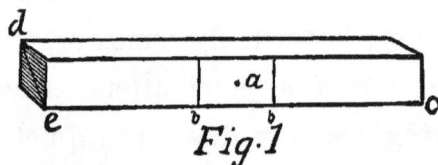

Fig. 1

from an oblong piece of wood like Fig. 1. Through the
center of this bore a hole, *a*, for the pivot upon which it
will finally turn, and mark the two lines at *b*. Now, commencing at the point *b*, cut off the corner, *b c*, and make

the surface flat as in Fig. 2 ; then cut off the opposite side
of the other end, indicated in Fig. 1 by the dotted lines

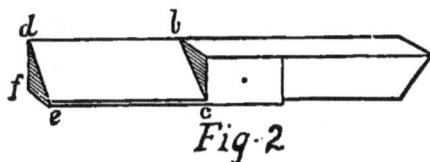

Fig. 2

d e, in a like manner. Your figure will now resemble Fig.
2, and both ends will form a prism like *b c d e f;* but *b
c d e* should be a thin flat blade, so the corner or edge,
commencing at *f*, should be cut down in the same manner
that *e d* was treated in Fig. 1. Make the other blade to
correspond and chamfer out the middle, or square piece,
as seen in Fig. 3. This middle piece is not a square, al-

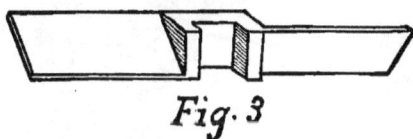

Fig. 3

though I have spoken of it as such, but is oblong, to allow
room for another two-bladed piece made precisely like
this to interlock with it. When these two pieces are
fitted together, fasten them with one or more nails, and
then insert the small round stick upon which the windmill is to turn. Fig. 4 shows an arrangement by which

two windmills are operated on the same stick. These
should turn in opposite directions to make them effective,
and this is easily accomplished by simply cutting the
vanes of the one so that the wind shall strike it at an
angle opposite to that with which it strikes the other.
Should you care to decorate them in colors, it had best
be done by painting bands or stripes across each vane, all
to correspond with each other in width and shade. For
instance, take the windmill in Fig. 4; let the outside
bands be of chrome yellow and one inch wide; the next

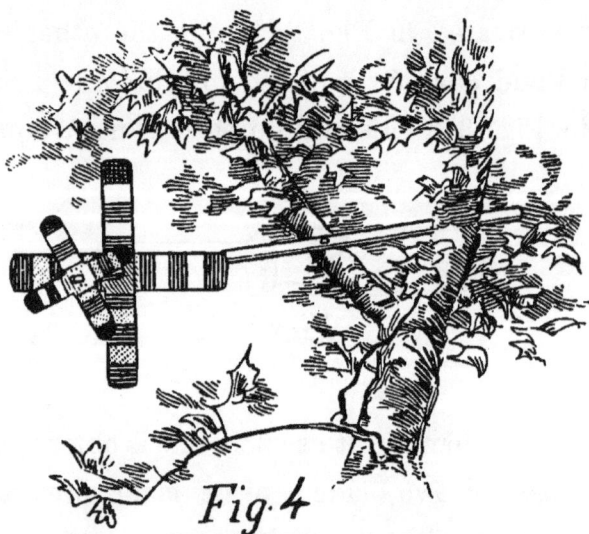

Fig. 4

red and two inches wide; while the third yellow, and the
fourth blue, should each be an inch in width. The axis

should have a greater diameter where the larger revolves upon it, but should be cut smaller where it meets the back of the little windmill. Nails in ·front and back of the

larger, and front of the smaller, are necessary to keep them in place.

Perhaps the most satisfactory way of arranging such a

windmill is to place it on the end of a weather-vane, as shown in Fig. 5. It is then always presented to the wind. The vane and the windmill may be painted the same color, or the latter may be decorated in stripes, as before described, and the vane given a color which will harmonize with it. Care must be exercised to fasten each part strongly in place, as the strain is very great during a strong wind or in a storm.

THE SCREW-PROPELLER; OR, WEATHER-VANE AND WIND-MILL COMBINED.

Take a piece of board, seven-eighths of an inch thick, and large enough to make a vessel of the size you desire.

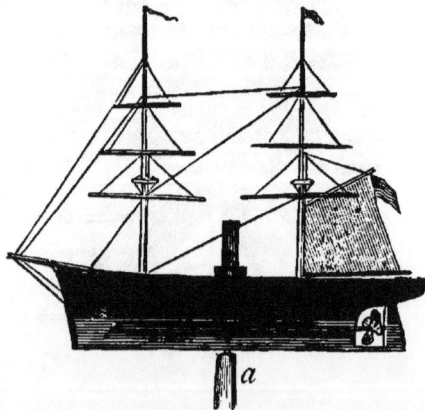

Cut out a hull like that in the illustration. Make a small windmill like that just described, but with rounded

ends to the vanes, like that represented in **Fig. 2.** **Pass**
a strong wire through the hole in the center, and drive
it into the stern of **Fig. 1**; fasten the
other end into the rudder, which should
be stationary. Be careful when planning
your vessel to allow sufficient room for
the windmill to revolve below the over
hang. Bore a hole at a for the pivot to rest in, upon
which the weather-vane is to turn, and insert the two
masts in their proper places. Cut a small mizzen-sail
from thin board and nail it to the mast.

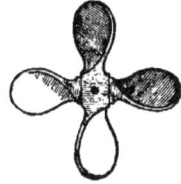

The flags are of red and blue flannel, the stays of
copper or galvanized wire, and the bowsprit a small
stick, cut from a tough bit of wood. This propeller may
be painted to suit the fancy, but usually is black, with a
narrow yellow or white stripe near the top. The lower
third is frequently painted green, however, which adds
considerably to its nautical appearance. The windmill
should be a bright red, and the entire vessel should have
plenty of time to dry before being placed in its final
position.

THE SIDE-WHEELER.

Another, and very pretty windmill, which can be easily
constructed by a boy, is in the form of a steam-boat, the
paddles of which are always presented to the wind by

the position of the boat itself. Cut out of a seven-eighths
of an inch board a hull like that seen in the illustration,
and make the hole for the pivot at the middle point between bow and stern ; bore another hole just aft of this
for the axle of the paddle-wheels.   Out of thin wood cut

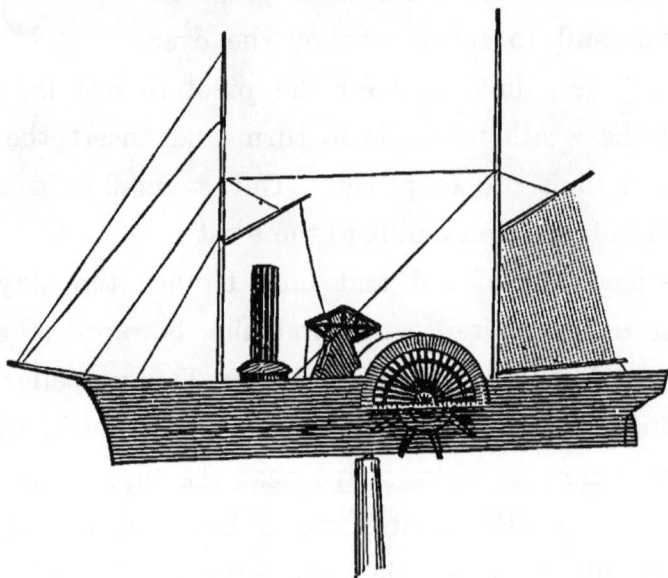

Fig. 1

two circular disks for these wheels, and dovetail the
paddles into their edges as seen in Fig. 2.   Next cut out
two half circles of your thin wood for paddle-boxes, and
bore a hole in each for the axle of the wheels.   These are
to shield the upper half of the wheels from the wind.
Now take a piece of tin, in shape like Fig. 3, and wide

enough to accommodate the wheels on either side, and
nail it to the edges of the paddle-boxes, as seen in the

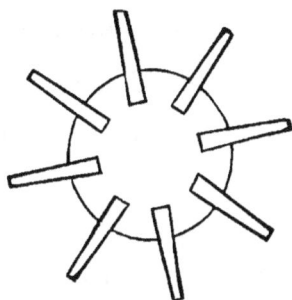

Fig. 2

figure ; the ends, *a*, are to be nailed upon the deck of the
steamer, and answer the purpose of keeping these boxes

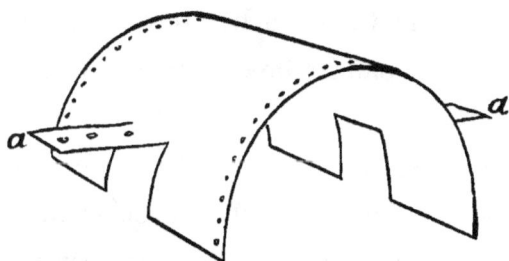

Fig. 3

in position. Paint this boat black and green, the latter
occupying the lower third of the hull, while a narrow
line of yellow or white around the top relieves the som-

berness of the upper part. The paddle-boxes should be
black, with narrow lines of light red radiating from a
small semicircular figure of the same color near the bottom. This boat should also be fitted with a small mizzen-
sail, made of tin or thin board, and painted white. The
top of the paddle-boxes is buff or light yellow, and the
wheels or windmills are a bright red.

In this steam-boat, a "dummy" walking-beam, cut out
of a single piece of thin wood, can be added if desired,
and should be painted in solid black, or, if liked, it can
be striped like that in the "Toy Steam-boat," elsewhere
described in this book. The smoke-stack in this, as well
as the screw-propeller, should be nailed in place before
the first painting.

If you should care to take the trouble, the walking-
beam can be made to move by simply cutting away the
hull between the paddle-boxes, to allow the crank to
turn in, and bending the axle of the wheels in the form
of the crank described in the "Toy Steam-boat." A
long slit must also be cut in the tin cover of the paddle-
boxes, to allow of the play of the connecting-rod. Small
flags of bright-colored strong cloth can be placed in the
proper places if desired, and really add considerable to
the bright, pretty effect when first made; but as they are
soon ruined by the combined influences of sun, rain, and
wind, they are hardly desirable, unless the boat is in

some position where it can be easily reached, and the little flags changed for new ones, as they become faded or torn.

THE REGATTA WINDMILL.

Take two sticks of wood, about three feet long, and one inch in diameter; fasten them together at their cen-

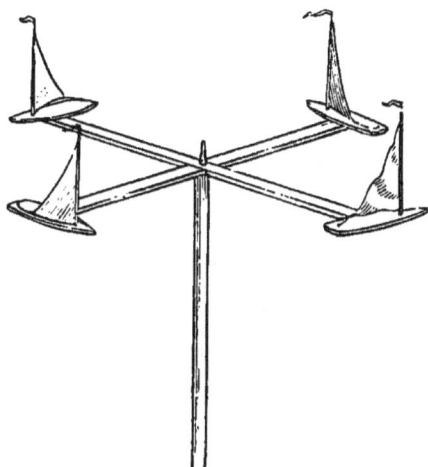

tral points, so that their arms shall be at right angles with each other (see Fig. 1); and bore a large hole through the point of intersection. From shingles cut out four boats, each eight inches long, and fit them with masts; next cut from strong new cloth four small triangular pieces for sails, and sew them to the masts; fasten the lower corner by a strong bit of cord to the stern, as seen in Fig. 2; then cut a small flag from red flannel and nail it to the top of the mast. You can paint these boats if you like, and also the cross-pieces upon which they are finally nailed. Care must be taken that they all head the same way. Observe their positions in Fig. 1.

Fig. 1 shows the affair finished and mounted on its pole. Place them in as high a position as possible, so that they may catch the breeze from all directions.

A BOY'S SOLAR MICROSCOPE.

The microscope is, as every boy knows, an optical instrument, which enables us to see and examine objects which are too small to be seen by the naked eye. The arrangement of the solar microscope is similar to that of the magic lantern, the sun taking the place of the lime-light usually employed. In this form of the magic lan-

tern, two difficulties are to be overcome ; one, the necessarily fixed position of the instrument ; and the other,
the very inconvenient habit the sun has of constantly
changing his position ; so that it would be impossible to
adjust the lens without the aid of a mirror, to throw sufficient light in upon the object to be examined. Both of
these obstacles are surmounted in the simple arrangement
of the solar microscope here described.

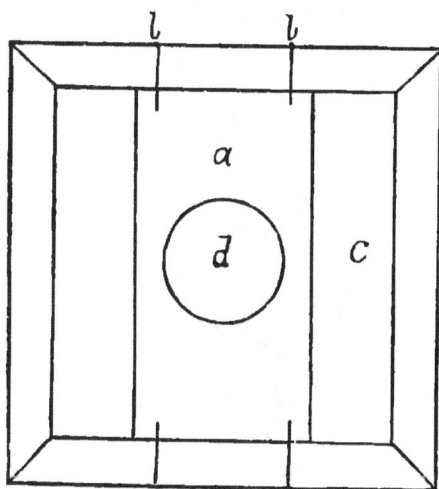

Fig. 1

First make a strong frame of wood, seven-eighths of an
inch in thickness, that will exactly fit in the lower half
of the window when the sash is thrown up ; and in the
middle of this fit an upright board a foot wide, which has
a hole cut in its center ten inches in diameter. Fasten it

strongly in place by four nails driven through the frame, and well into the ends of the boards, or, if more convenient, by long screws inserted in the same places. Fig. 1 shows the position of the board *a*, also that of the nails *b*. The open spaces, *c*, are to be closed by several thicknesses of brown paper pasted or tacked across on the inside

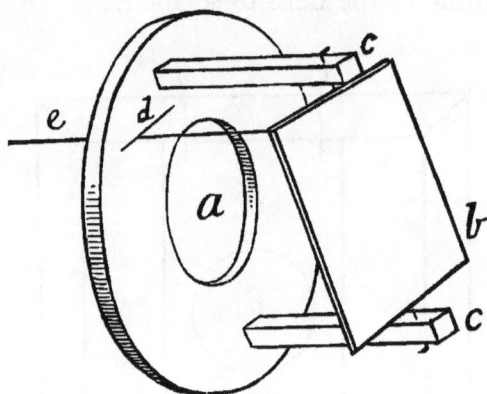

Fig. 2

of the frame. The upper part of the window must also be closed, so that no ray of light shall enter the room, except through the hole *d*.

Before proceeding further, it may be well to remark, that, as perhaps the largest part of the work is the cutting of no less than seven circular holes of various sizes, through as many pieces of board, a scroll-saw will be

found an almost indispensable aid to the construction
of this apparatus. Also, that the window in which this
microscope is used must necessarily have a southern
exposure.

In Fig. 2 we have a disk of half-inch wood, twelve
inches in diameter, with an opening in the center four
inches across, to hold the condensing lens, *a ; b* is a mirror five inches wide and ten inches long, turning on an axis
which passes through the supports, *c c*, the latter being attached to the disk. These supports should be long enough
to admit of the mirror turning entirely around without
touching the disk, and are fastened in place by screws
passing through the disk and into their ends. When the

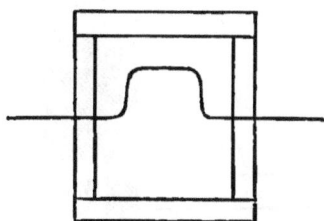

Fig. 3

mirror is in place, cut the slit *d* parallel with the edge of
the mirror, for the wire *e* to pass through. The manner
of attaching the wire to the back of the mirror is seen in
Fig. 3. The back is first covered with paper to prevent

its scratching ; then the wire is bent and laid in place,
and lastly, a piece of very strong paper is pasted over

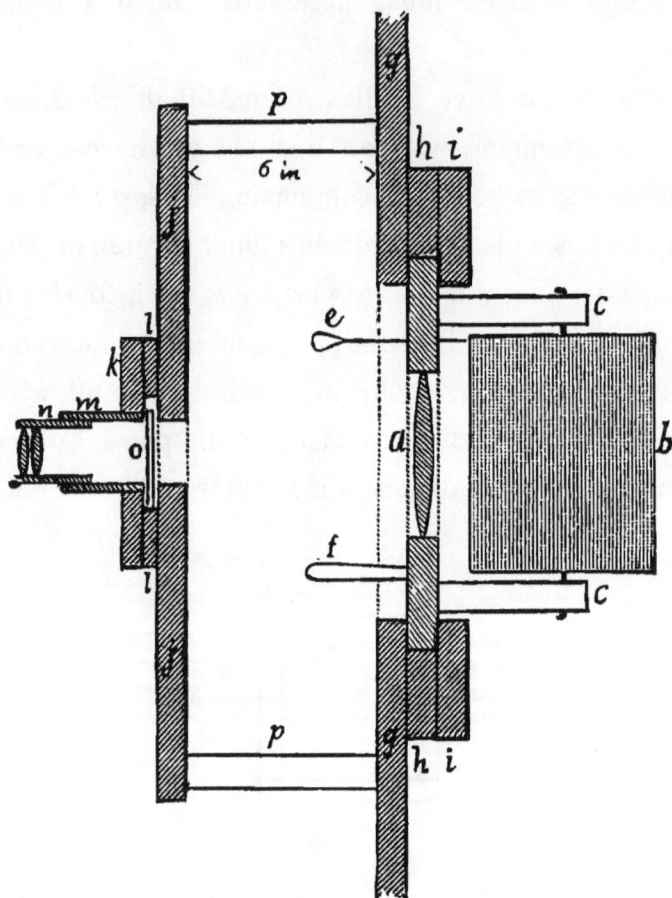

Fig. 4

the wire and entire back, and caught down over the edge
of the front, forming a narrow frame to the glass ; the
ends of this wire should pass through rather small holes

in *c c*, so that it will not turn easily out of position. A handle (see *f*, Fig. 4) should be placed on the other side of the disk, and just across the lens from the slit *d*.

Next take two pieces of wood, fifteen inches square and half an inch thick ; in the center of one cut a hole twelve inches in diameter, while in that of the other cut another round hole only ten inches across. In Fig. 4, which represents a section of this microscope, *g* is the central board of the screen, marked *a* in Fig. 1 ; *h* is the piece you have just made, with the central opening twelve inches in diameter ; and *i* is the second piece, which measures fifteen inches square, but has a hole of only ten inches diameter in its center ; *d*, which has a dotted surface, to distinguish it from the frame-work, is the large disk (Fig. 2), which, you remember, is just twelve inches in diameter, and, consequently, will exactly fit the opening in *h ;* if these edges are rough, sand-paper both with a coarse quality first, finishing them off with a finer kind. When *d* is in position, and moves easily but not loosely in *h*, place *i* over it and fasten it in place with screws, passing through *i* into *h ;* but *h*, of course, must first be strongly nailed or screwed upon *g*.

You will now see that by turning the handle, *f*, the position of the mirror, which is fastened to this disk, can be easily changed so that it shall face in any direction, while by drawing the wire, *e*, it can be turned so as to reflect the sun's rays through the lens, *a*, from whatever quarter of the heavens it may be shining. This double adjustment of the mirror and lens enables you to throw the rays of the sun through the opening in upon the object, *o*, at any hour of the day. As the mirror is adjusted in Fig. 4, the sun must be very low, as its rays, to strike the mirror, would necessarily be nearly horizontal.

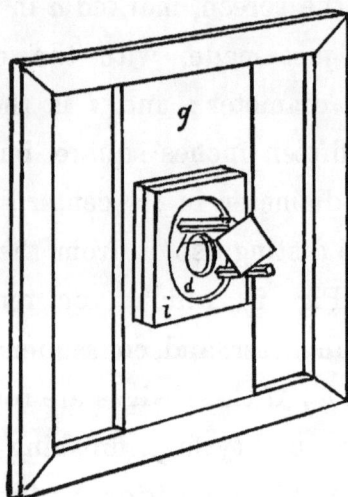

Fig. 5

The lens, *a*, should be held in place by two pieces of whalebone, bent around on either side of it, at the edge of the opening in *d;* this lens is four inches in diameter, and has a focal length of nine or ten inches; its adjustment had better be left till everything else in the microscope has been finished.   Fig. 5 shows the appearance of this when completed.

As the outer part of the work is fitted, we will now turn our attention to the other, or inner, side of the screen.   In Fig. 4, the board *j* is eighteen inches long

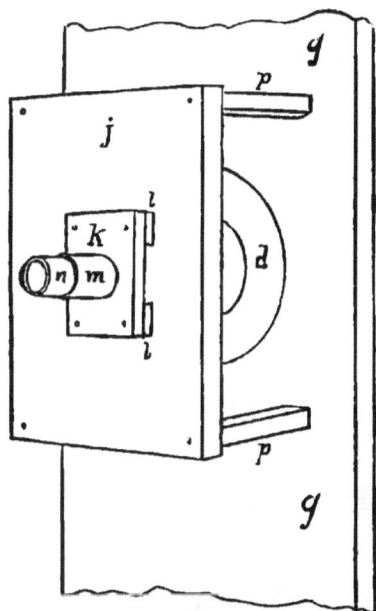

Fig. 6

by ten inches wide, and half-an-inch thick.   In the middle is a small circular hole, one and one-half inches in diameter.   This is fastened to the middle board, *g*, by the four horizontal posts, *p*, each six inches long.

Now take a square piece of half-inch board, five

inches across, cut a circular hole two inches in diameter in the middle, and fit into this hole a pasteboard tube four inches long, which is painted black on the inside. The edge of the circular hole in *j* should also be black. In Fig. 6, which represents this board, you will notice two cleats, *l l*, fastened to the back of *k*; these are also made of half-inch wood, and are five inches long by one wide. In Fig. 4, the position of *k* and *l* is seen in connection with the longer piece, *j*; the center of the openings in *j* and *k* should form one and the same horizontal line. The opening between *l* and *l* is for the glass slides upon which the objects to be examined are placed.

After these parts are fastened in their proper places, make a pasteboard tube, with a black inner surface, as represented at *n*, about four inches in length, and inclose in one end two lenses, each one and one-half inches in diameter, and each having a focal length of four inches. Fit this tube in the one marked *m*. Now, having everything in place, fit in the lens, *a*, so that it will send the rays of light directly through the hole in *j* upon the object in *l*, and fasten it securely in place with your bent whalebones.

The screen upon which the image is thrown can be the opposite whitewashed surface of the room, if by a proper adjustment of the tubes the image can be made distinct, or it can be a sheet stretched over a frame-work of light wood; the latter is preferable, as it can be more easily brought in focus. Of course, in this form, as in any other "magic lantern," the nearer the screen to the lantern, the longer the tubes *m n;* but the image, which is smaller, gains in brilliancy of illumination, while with these conditions reversed, the results are the opposite; a larger image, but less bright in appearance. The same light being spread over a larger surface is necessarily less strong.

SOME OBJECTS FOR THIS MICROSCOPE.

The objects which can be examined by aid of this instrument are many in number, and can be readily prepared by simply inserting them between two pieces of glass, sufficiently small to slide in the opening *l l*, and pasting bits of brown paper over the edges to hold them in place.

In this manner the legs of flies and mosquitoes, the heads of the latter with their venomous sting; hairs of the dog and cat, also from the human head; tiny sections of human skin; down from the butterfly's wing, obtained by dusting off a few of the tiny particles upon a glass plate; the pollen from different flowers; spores of the puff-ball and tiny grains of dust, all make very interesting subjects for study, when magnified and thrown upon the screen in the darkened room.

8

One of the most interesting experiments with this form of the magic lantern is made by throwing the image of a drop of some solution, like sulphate of copper, upon the screen, and watching the process of its crystallization; sulphate of copper and of iron; hyposulphite of soda, which latter may be colored by adding a very little permanganate of potash to the solution.

The eels in a drop of vinegar, drops of stagnant water, and the larvæ of the mosquito are also interesting objects, when viewed by the aid of this powerful magnifier.

SEA-MOSSES.

No boy who has lived on our coast, or, indeed, who has spent much time near the sea, could have failed to notice and admire the beautiful feathery mosses which sway about so gracefully under the surface of the water. The most delicate mosses are not found upon the open sea-beach, but in the more sheltered bays and inlets near the coast, and one who has never given them especial attention cannot fail to be impressed by the great variety of form and color to be found within a small space of water. Ranging in color from the palest pink or straw to the deepest purple or brown, and from the lightest sea-green to the darkest shade of olive, they are capable of being arranged in most beautiful bits of coloring, while the delicate, fine specimens, united with the coarser varieties, add to the effectiveness of the whole. To gather and arrange these mosses is not as difficult a task as most people imagine. Any boy can, with a little care, make a fine collection, which would be valued very highly by some inland friend who cannot reach the sea-shore every year, or perhaps not more than once or twice in a lifetime. If any of you, my boy readers, have any such friend, do not fail to collect a quantity of the mosses common to the waters near you, and arrange them on cards for their preservation. In gathering your mosses have an old tin can filled with water in the bottom of the boat, and after detaching from the stones, throw them immediately into the can. When you get home they can be left in the can of salt water over night, if you have not the time to attend to them at once; or they may be put into a basin of fresh water, and left for awhile to wash away the salt and sand that remains on them. When they seem perfectly clean, take two or three carefully up on a bit of paper and throw them into a basin of clean water.

Now the delicate part of the process is reached. Have a number of square pieces of unglazed paper at hand— ribbon paper is very good for the purpose—and thrust them carefully into the water under the bit of moss you desire to take out. With a long, slender darning-needle

carefully arrange the tiny filaments, so that they shall
form a graceful composition, and raise the card carefully
from the water.   It is not necessary to exercise as much
care with the coarser "silver mosses," as their more wiry
branchlets naturally assume graceful positions, and the

water flowing from the surface of the card does not so
easily disarrange their positions.   When all the mosses
have been taken up on cards, fasten each to a table or
shelf to dry.   This is done by driving a pin through one

corner of the card into the edge of the shelf or table, and
allowing it to remain undisturbed until both the moss and
paper are perfectly dry. They may now be mounted
upon cards prepared for the purpose, and their names,

with the locality where they were found, neatly written
beneath ; or they may be preserved in a case or frame.

The illustrations show two different arrangements of
sea-mosses for the frame. In the first, that seen in Fig.
1, they are glued upon a background of fine white card-

board, one layer superimposed above another, until they extend forward from the card for an inch or more. Their stems are finally covered by a small, well-striped scallop-shell which has been washed clean and varnished. It is perhaps needless to add that the effect is very pretty. The "silver mosses" are best adapted for this arrangement.

The design given in Fig. 2 is quite grotesque in its appearance, and appeals rather more to the average boy's taste than the former arrangement. Red and brown mosses are used entirely, unless the effect seems too somber, in which case a little "silver moss" may be introduced on the back to lighten it a trifle.

Tiny baskets, made of pretty scallop-shells nicely fitted together and varnished, are often filled with the coarser varieties of moss, and are very pretty; but if they are unprotected from the dust they are soon destroyed, and unless covered with a glass case or inverted thin plain glass tumbler, they hardly pay for the trouble of making.

ANTIQUES AND HORRIBLES.

This is another of the mechanical toys which was common during my childhood. The whole affair is so simple that a small boy could make it, in a less finished form at

least, and the most sullen little fellow in all the land could not fail to be amused by the grotesque procession of clowns and hobgoblins, kings and countrymen, birds and fishes and animals, whose names no naturalist could tell, and whose like was never seen on this earth before. This procession travels on and on, as long as the crank is turned. The above illustration gives some idea of a few of the many members of the band, but any boy at all ingenious, will see that he has a variety—the more grotesque and outlandish the better the effect. Fig. 2 shows a section of the machinery ; the box-like covering is removed, and the frame-work exposed to view. First procure a board, *a*, about twenty by eight inches ; next two rollers upon which the band is to turn, for you must have seen that these little images are made of thin cardboard, attached to an endless band of strong cloth. These rollers should be rather larger than broomsticks, and held in place by four uprights, *c*. Only two of these can be seen in the cut. A table, *d e*, extends between the rollers and is supported by four legs, *f*, which should be of sufficient length to make the top, *d e*, come just below the upper section of the band. *g g* are boards, the same width as the bottom, *a*, and of sufficient height to make a good foundation for the top, and to allow free passage of the procession. None of the figures should be much over three inches in height, and none should be attached to

the cloth in more than one place; that is, by only one
foot, as they would be unavoidably torn in passing over
the rollers if more firmly fixed.   The top and front are of

pasteboard, and the whole exposed surface is covered
with pretty wall-paper.   On the right roller at the back
end, fix a small crank, or handle, and the machine is
started by turning this.   When about to give a grand
exhibition, be careful to turn in the right direction, and
not set the whole procession running backward, as you
might easily do if unobserving or forgetful.   The images
are much more amusing if painted in bright colors.   Use
plenty of blue, red, yellow, black, and white paint, with
a touch here and there of rich green and purple ; and you
may perhaps almost make your audience believe that
Fourth of July is here again, and they are viewing the
"Antiques and Horribles" through the large end of a
spy-glass.

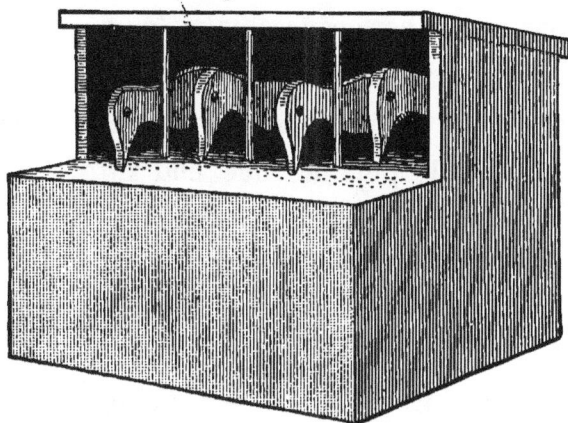

Fig. 1

THE MUSICAL CHICKENS.

One of the most pleasing toys for children, which may be counted among those made by boys themselves, is this little coop of chickens. Make a box like Fig. 1, leaving off the top and back boards until the works are placed within it. The little bars which separate the chickens are thin strips of wood. In Fig. 2, *a* represents one of the chickens, which is also made of thin wood and painted yellow; a hole is made at *b*, to allow the passage of a strong stiff wire, upon which the chickens turn, and by which they are also kept in place. At the end, *c*, of each, a strong piece of linen thread is tied through a small hole bored for the purpose, and each line is caught to a separate nail, driven in the bottom of the box, just below the chicken, in such a manner that when it is drawn tightly in place it will just touch the roller *d*. Fig. 1 shows just where each chicken is placed, and how far their heads protrude through the bars. The ends of the wire, *b*, which holds them in place, can be fastened on one side by simply pushing one end into a hole bored

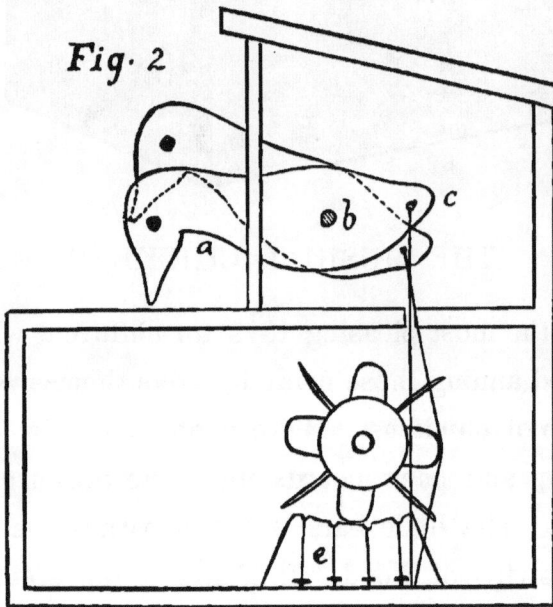

Fig. 2

partly through the wood to receive it ; the other should be slipped into a groove made for it, and fastened in place by a wedge nailed just above it when in position. Fig. 3 shows the roller in full, and the little blocks or cams which are placed along its surface. These little cams are made of wood, not more than three-eighths of an

inch thick, and are placed at such distances from each
other along the roller that the middle point of each shall
come opposite one of the threads.

Between these blocks, but so situated that they will
not come in contact with any one of the threads, are little
quills, driven into tiny gashes made in the roller. These
quills are an inch long, and should all be of the same
length. One end of the roller is fitted with a crank, while
the other is fastened in place by a wooden pin or long nail.
Below this, at either end of the box, is a curved bridge, *e,*

Fig. 3

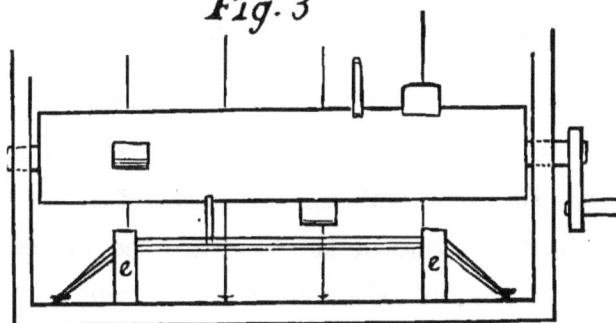

into which grooves are cut and slender brass wires drawn
very tightly, as seen in a violin. The curve made by the
wires, however, is unlike that in the above-named instrument, being concave instead of convex. Now it will be
seen that by placing the roller in such a position that the
quills will strike the wires with some force as the wheel
revolves, a constant tinkling sound like that of a toy piano

is the result; and at the same time, as the little blocks come in contact with the strings, they push the thread backward, and in so doing lower the point *c*, and consequently raise the head of the chicken. The top of the extension in front of the bars is made of thin board and painted green, while a slight sprinkling of yellow over its surface represents the meal the chickens are supposed to be eating. The remainder of the box may be painted to suit the fancy of the maker.

CAPTAIN S.'S PEG PUZZLE.

One bright summer morning, which seems but a short while ago, unless I stop and count the years that have passed since then, we children were invited to take a sail across the bay with one of the kind-hearted old captains who owned a trim little cat-boat, which her owner was wont to boast would beat any other craft of her length in the harbor. But there was not much chance of beating anything on the morning of which I write, for, although a light northerly breeze was stirring when we intended to start, the girls of our party took so much time in which to get ready, that by the time we were fairly under way we were scarcely able to fill our sail. However, we managed to make some little headway, and in the course of two hours reached the beautiful rocky point covered with its grove of fine old trees, which, but for the delay in starting, would have been reached much earlier in the day. This point was quite a favorite spot for excursionists, and was hailed with delight by most of our party. We boys, however, cared more for the little *Sea Dog*, and the companionship of old Captain S., than for the walks on shore. So, claiming our full share of the good things packed in the baskets stowed away in the cabin, we decided to remain on board and share our picnic with the captain on the bay.

After all were on shore, and the hampers had been taken to the grove, we hoisted the sail and made for deeper water; but there was no wind, and we had to content ourselves with looking at the glassy surface around us, and feeling that we were in a boat away from shore, even if not in rapid motion. We ate our lunch as we listened to a delightful story told by the captain, of how his ship was once chased by a pirate, and only escaped through the timely interposition of a snow-storm. We next tried our hands at the oars and rowed some distance further from the land. Finally, as we were about to return for the others of our party on shore, a small piece of wood Fred found on the cabin floor changed the current of our thoughts, and we saw for the first time the little device I am about to describe. This bit of wood.

which he had picked up was a thin strip of a cigar-box cover. In one end was a circular hole about an inch in diameter, in the middle was a square hole of the same diameter, and at the extreme end was still another opening, in the form of an isosceles triangle, the perpendicular being of the same length as the side of the square.

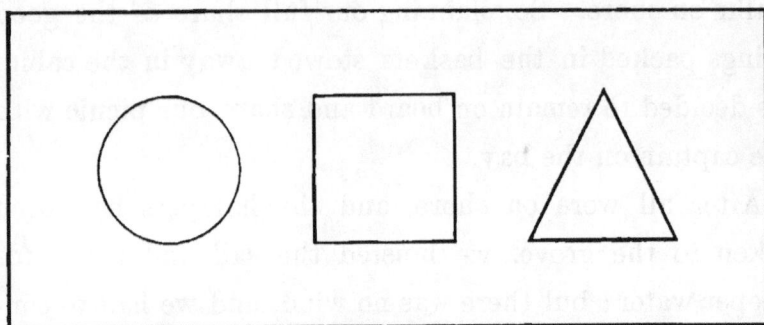

Fig. 1

When Captain S. saw the piece of wood he challenged us each to make one peg which should exactly fit all three holes. "But it can't be done, Captain," we both exclaimed at once ; "the holes that have corners couldn't be fitted with a round peg, and the peg large enough for the square would be too large for the triangle," continued Fred, as he examined the openings more carefully. "But it can be done," answered Captain S., with a peculiar kind of chuckle he always gave when very much pleased. "It can be done, for I have done it hundreds of times."

He had done it hundreds of times; had made one peg which should fit a round, a square, and a triangular hole, and fit them nicely! How was it to be done? We thought it over, and tried to study it out; we even took out our jackknives and whittled away at an old broken thole-pin which lay in the bottom of the boat. But we couldn't make it work; there were always the corners to be filled, and little spaces would be left if we tried to compromise, and make the pin less round as it increased in length; then the triangle! that wouldn't accommodate itself to any shape we could devise. We whittled away for over an hour, now and again receiving a little encouragement from the captain, who greatly enjoyed our successive failures. During the meantime a brisk south-west wind had sprung up, and we were bounding over the water at a delightful speed; but we paid little attention to the sail; in fact, we hardly knew we were moving at all, so intent had we become to solve the mystery. After the others of the party came on board, we soon fired them with our enthusiasm, and every bit of available wood and every jackknife was brought into use. But not one of the party was bright enough to hit upon the right shape. I shall never forget the fun made of us by the girls—not one of whom, by the way, could sharpen a lead-

pencil decently—when the captain finally showed us how
the thing was done. Asking one of the older boys to
take the helm, he picked up a bit of wood we had thrown
aside as too small, whipped out his jackknife, and in less
time than it takes me to write it, had the peg made and
fitted to the holes. How he made it fit so well in so short
a time has never ceased to be a source of wonder to me;
but probably the practice of years, while off on lonely
whaling cruises, had something to do with his dexterity.

He first whittled out a cylinder, which exactly fitted
the circular hole; then he cut it off, so that its length
should be the same as the diameter of the square (see
Fig. 2). Now, by putting this sideways into the square

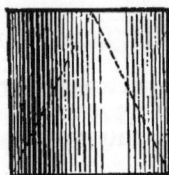      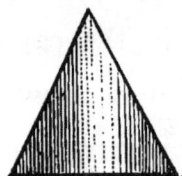

Fig. 2   *Fig. 3*   *Fig. 4*

opening, it fitted it perfectly. Lastly, leaving the base of
the cylinder undisturbed, he cut away from either side
until he had a shape like Fig. 3, which, when looked at
from another point, presents the appearance of Fig. 4,
and would, of course, perfectly fit the last and triangular
opening.

SLATE GAMES FOR CHILDREN.

A slate is one of the most useful presents which can be given to a child. Long before the little hands can fashion letters, or the infant mind comprehend them, the baby fingers can make marks and scratches upon the smooth surface and derive considerable amusement from the exercise.

As the little one grows older, these meaningless scrawls gradually change to more intelligible forms, and then it is that the " Tit-Tat-To," so very old, and yet so delightfully new, to every little girl or boy in their turn, comes into play.

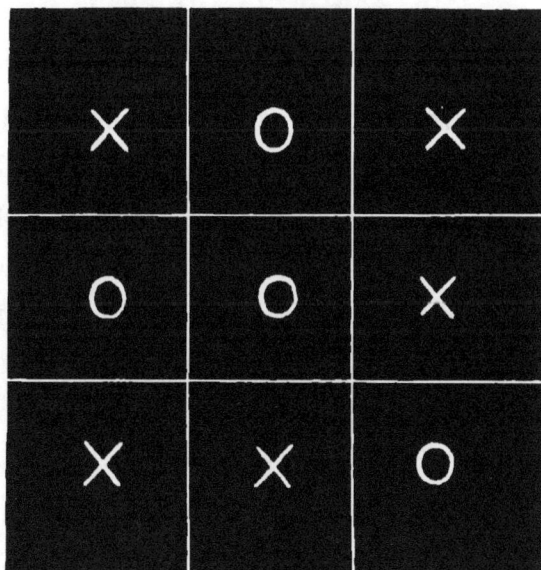

TIT-TAT-TO.

This game is played on a figure similar to the above,

made on an ordinary slate. The players alternately mark
in the figure, the one a cross, and the other a nought; he
who first obtains a row, either horizontally, perpendicu-
larly, or diagonally, wins the game, and calls out the following rhyme:

"Tit-Tat-To, my last go;
Three jolly butchers all in a row."

The object of each of the players is equally to obtain
such a row and to prevent his opponent from obtaining
one.

AIR, EARTH, OR THE SEA?

This game—which is sometimes called *Birds, Beasts,
and Fishes*—is instructive as well as interesting to children who have some slight knowledge of natural history.
It is played as follows: Two boys take their slates, and
each writes down the first and last letters of the name of
some bird, beast, or fish; first stating whether it belongs
to the air, earth, or water, or from which category the
name is selected, and puts a cross for each of the inter-
mediate letters.   For example: James writes upon his
slate T × × × r, and remarks, as he passes it to his companion, "the earth."   Charles selects a bird and marks
upon his slate as follows: E × × × e, saying, at the same
time, "the air."   They exchange slates, and each tries to

guess the name of the beast or bird indicated, and fills
up the blanks accordingly. It is evident that those indicated above are respectively tiger and eagle.

TURKS AND RUSSIANS.

The slate should be divided into three divisions, the

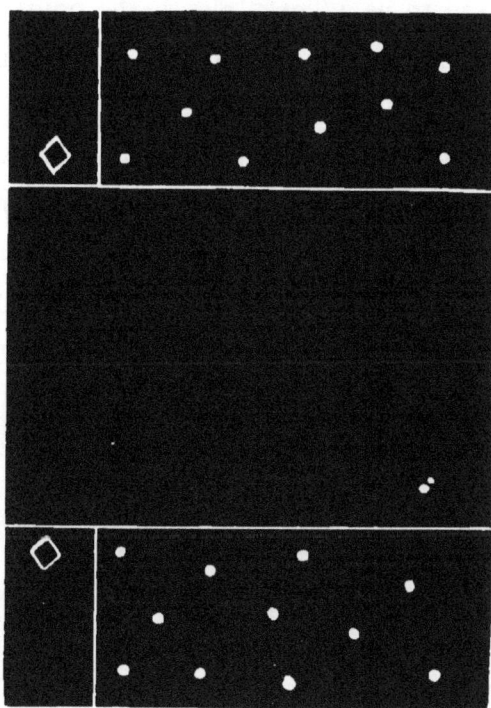

top and bottom divisions each having a small compartment marked off therein, as shown in the annexed
diagram.

One of the two end divisions should be allotted to the
Turks, and the other to the Russians, and marks put
therein, to represent the soldiers of the respective nations.

Each player having provided himself with a well-
sharpened pencil, the game is played as follows : The
players decide the order of play, and the first selected
being supposed to be a Turk, places the point of his pencil at the spot marked in the smaller compartment of the
Turkish division of the slate and draws it quickly across
the slate in the direction of the opposing army.

The pencil will, of course, leave a line marking its
track, and all the men of the opposite side through which
the track passes count as dead. Each player plays alternately, and he wins who first kills all the men on the
opposite side.

The track of the pencil must be rapidly made and must
be either straight or curved ; any track in which there is
an angle does not count. Sometimes the players turn
their heads or close their eyes when making the track.

THIRTY-ONE.

Although this game is usually played upon a board
similar to the one in the cut, and with small wooden
blocks made for the purpose, a slate properly marked off

would answer very well for the board, and bits of pasteboard, marked with the necessary figures, do equally well for the blocks.

The game consists of playing these bricks or squares of pasteboard, so that the column added up makes just thirty-one.

As only two persons play together, suppose William

and Mary are contestants. Mary commences the game by playing a six; that is, she slides one of the blocks numbered six over to the right-hand side of the board. Then William plays block No. 4. This makes ten. Mary then plays two, and William follows with a five, making seventeen total. Now, some calculation is necessary if either will win. Mary, after some study, ventures a five, and William plays a six. It is now only necessary for Mary to slide No. 3 over to the right side, to make the total thirty-one and beat.

That move of Mary's—which was made after considerable deliberation—was not a safe one, as William could have moved over a one and made the total only twenty-three. This would require eight more to complete the required thirty-one, and as six is the largest number on the blocks, William would have had the last play and gained the contest.

Rules for Thirty-one.

The object of each player is to gain thirty-one, or *nearer* thirty-one than his opponent, *without going over* that number.

Put the blocks or bits of pasteboard on the left side of the board; and each in turn moves any piece they like to the other side.

Each player moves alternately one piece at a time.

Add together the numbers on *all the blocks moved*, until one or the other gains thirty-one, without going over that number.

The player gaining this number by his individual block wins.

The final honor is given to him who wins three out of five single games.

SOLITAIRE.

During the long winter evenings, we cannot have too many games to amuse the younger members of the household, and a variety is always acceptable.

Where the family is large and the means small, and especially in the country where boys are forced to rely upon their own devices in the way of amusement, few of the ready-made games find their way into the household.

Now boys, and girls, too, let me whisper to you so softly that your city cousins may not hear—you are no losers because of that fact. A great part of the enjoyment of a thing consists in the making of it. And many of the games which are best enjoyed by children all over the land you can, with a little ingenuity and some trouble, perhaps, make for yourself.

Among the many things which a boy can make, there are very few more interesting or fascinating than the simple game of Solitaire, or, as it is more frequently called, *The Peg Puzzle.*

Take a piece of smooth board, from nine inches to a foot square, cut out the corners as indicated in the illustration, and bore holes in the positions indicated by the dots.

Out of soft pine or other suitable wood whittle thirty-two pegs, which are to fit into these holes ; the middle or thirty-third hole is to be left empty.

The game consists in removing all the pegs excepting one from the board, and that one is to be left in the middle hole.

This is effected, as in " checkers," by a series of capt-

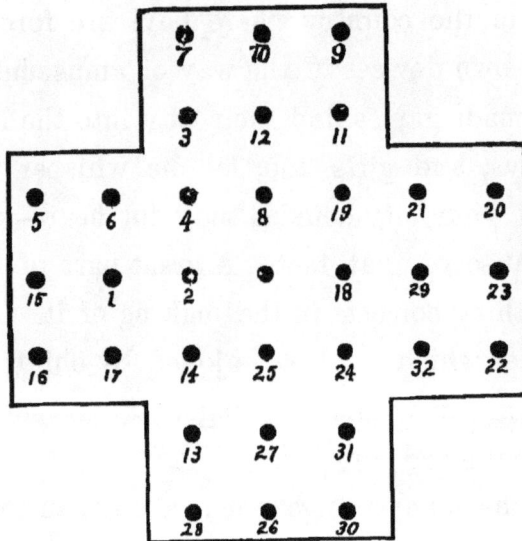

ures ; that is, when taken off the board, the peg removed must first have been jumped over by another peg.

In beginning the game, peg No. 1 jumps over peg No. 2, and is placed in the central hole. No. 2 is then removed from the board. As the hole occupied by No. 2 is now empty, peg No. 3 jumps over No. 4, and is placed in the empty hole No. 2. No. 4 is removed, and the moves continue in like manner as those described.

The following is a key to the solution of the puzzle, but should not be consulted until you find it impossible to accomplish the feat without its aid.

KEY.

1 to centre	6 to 8	20 to 19
3 to 2	13 to 2	11 to 18
5 to 4	x to 1	24 to 14
2 to 3	15 to 2	26 to 25
7 to 4	16 to 14	25 to 17
8 to 6	2 to 13	28 to 14
9 to 7	18 to 11	17 to 25
11 to 3	20 to 19	29 to x
7 to 4	8 to 21	x to 27
	22 to 20	30 to 24
		32 to 25
		27 to centre.

BATTLEDORE AND SHUTTLECOCK.

If any of my young boy friends wishes to make a useful, and at the same time acceptable, present to a sister or girl friend, he cannot do better than make a set of this pretty and amusing game.

The battledore is readily made with a hickory stick and a piece of hoop, and the shuttlecock with a cork and

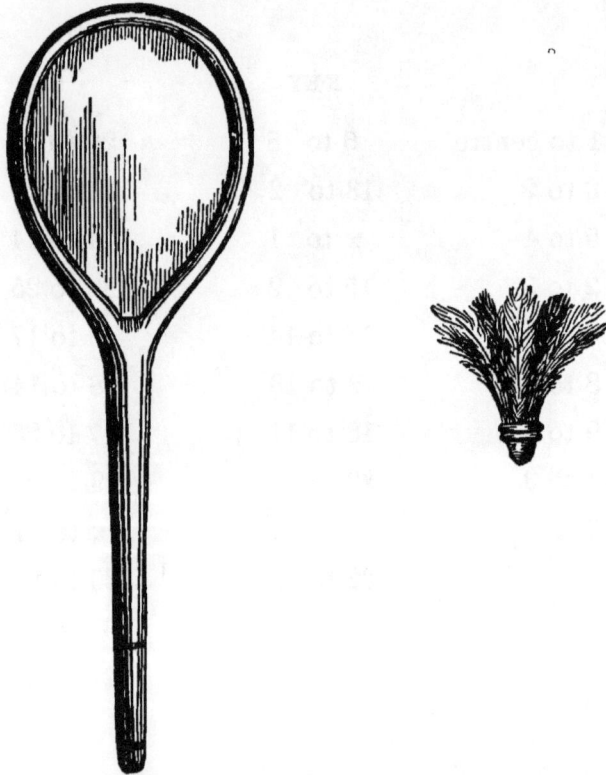

a few short feathers.   The forms of the two are shown in the illustrations.

The game is played by two players, each having a battledore, and each bats the shuttlecock from one to the

other, the one failing to return it when it is batted to him within possible reach losing a point in the game. A game consists of twenty points, and the best two out of three games gains the match.

RING TOSS.

This light pastime for the summer lawn, or for the parlor on a winter's evening, is one of the most graceful and pretty games ever invented. Although particularly intended for the fairer sex, boys are generally the most skillful, if not the most graceful, competitors in the game.

This game is played with a target-post, more or less ornamental, as the skill and taste of the maker may decree, and a number of light rings or small hoops, ranging from five to ten inches in diameter.

The rings are nicely made of old hoop-skirt wires, bent in the desired shape, and strongly fastened with cords, the whole covered with bright silk or ribbon ; the greater variety of colors used the brighter the effect of the game. The ribbons need not necessarily be perfectly fresh, as in winding the rings any soiled spots can readily be hidden.

It is also better to have the rings divided into three sets or sizes, and all those of each set as nearly as possible of the same size. For instance, if eighteen rings are to be used, let six be about five inches in diameter, six more be seven or eight inches, and the remaining six to be ten inches across.

The game is simply to toss the rings so as to fall on the target-post. The smaller the rings the higher the count.

For the large rings one point is scored, for the next in size two points, and for the smallest or five-inch rings, three points—fifty points being a full game.

The distance on a lawn which the player stands from the target-post is twenty-five feet. In the parlor it is fifteen feet.

CHECKERS.

As I write the above title, I wonder if there is a boy or a girl in this great American land who does not own a checker-board, or does not know how to play this delightful game. The game was brought to us from England, we cannot say how many years ago, probably by the first settlers in these then lonely wilds.

This game of checkers is a scientific one and is governed entirely by calculation. So, in order to become a good player, one has to give considerable time and thought to the subject, which is perhaps as good mental discipline as many of our less interesting school studies.

The game is played upon a board or table, divided off into thirty-two white and thirty-two black squares, with twelve white and twelve black men or checkers.

The board can be made out of thin wood, or upon a

strong piece of pasteboard, the white squares left the original color of the material used, and the black colored with ink or paint, whichever is most conveniently at hand.

9

For the checkers, small pieces of wood may be used, or black and white buttons be substituted in their place.

The table or board should be so placed that each player shall have a black square at his right hand, if playing on the white squares, or a white square, if playing on the black.

The men move obliquely *forward* until they arrive at the last, or the adversary's head row, when they are made kings and can then move *backward* as well as *forward*.

To distinguish a king from a common man he is crowned, by placing another checker of the same color on top of him, as soon as he reaches the *king's row.*

The adversary's men are taken by leaping over them, and *must be taken* whenever offered or exposed. No move can be recalled after the man has been quitted; that is, after the finger has been removed from him.

The players have the first move in each game alternately.

Checkers may best be learned by playing, for awhile at least, upon a board on which the white squares are numbered, some authorities advising the placing of permanent numbers in a corner of each white square, so as to be seen when the men are placed.

The numbers are arranged as follows: 1 being on your right hand and 4 on your left; number 5 the right hand of the second row, and 8 the left, and so on. See illustration.

The black men are placed upon 1 to 12 ; the white on 21 to 32.

In order to understand the game more readily, it may be of some assistance to beginners to show how a simple game might be played.

Suppose B., who has the black men, makes the first move from 11 to 15. W. follows him with 22 to 18. B. now moves from 15 to 22, jumping over 18, and capturing it by the move. 22 is now exposed, so W. is obliged to take it, and to do so moves from 25 to 18. B. now commences a new line of moving, and passes 8 to 11. W. moves 29 to 25 thus breaking his king's row. B. 4 to 8 ; W. 25 to 22 ; B. 12 to 16 ; W. 24 to 20 ; B. 10 to 15. Now W. moves 27 to 24, and loses the game by so doing. B. follows with 16 to 19, thus exposing 19. As it is a law in the game that the opposite side must take up the exposed men, W. is obliged to jump 19, and moves from 23 to 16 in so doing. B. moves from 15 to 19; W. 24 to 15 to jump 19 ; B. 9 to 14; W. 18 to 9, and captures 14. B. now sees 15 and 22 exposed, and moves from 11 to 25, thus capturing both men by the act. W. 32 to 27 ; B. 5 to 14, jumping 9. W. 27 to 23 ; B. 6 to 10. W. 16 to 12 ; B. 8 to 11. W. 28 to 24 ; B. 25 to 29, and is made a king. W. now moves 30 to 25, but as 29 is a king and can move backward as well as forward, B. moves from 29 to 22 and jumps 25, but exposes the king, which is quickly captured by W., who moves from 26 to 17. Now both sides proceed in a quiet manner for a time, B. moving from 11 to 15, W. 20 to 16, B. 15 to 18, W. 24 to 20. B. captures 23 by moving from 18 to 27, and W. takes 27 by jumping from 31 to 24. B. 14 to 18 ; W. 16 to 11, which is taken by B. who moves 7 to 16. W., in turn, takes 16 with 20, which he jumps over to 11. B. 18 to 23 ; W. 11 to 8. B. 23 to 27, and

Fig. 1　　　　　　　　　　　Fig. 2

W. now gains another king by moving 8 to 4. B. moves 27 to 31 and also gets a king. The king, you remember, can move backward, so W. moves from 4 to 8 ; B. 31 to 27. W. 24 to 20 ; B. 27 to 23. W. 8 to 11 ; B. 23 to 18. W. 11 to 8, and B. 18 to 15, which shows the game is lost to W.

The two following problems are given for practice, and are intended to materially assist the learner in gaining some knowledge of the intricacies of the game.

SOLUTION TO NO. 1.		SOLUTION TO NO. 2.	
Black to move and win.		White to move and win.	
Black.	**White.**	**White.**	**Black.**
1st move 6 to 1	5 to 9	1st move 18 to 14	5 to 1
2d move 10 to 15	9 to 5	2d move 14 to 9	1 to 5
3d move 15 to 18	5 to 9	3d move 22 to 17	5 to 14
4th move 1 to 5	9 to 6	4th move 17 to 10	21 to 25
5th move 18 to 15	21 to 17	5th move 10 to 15	25 to 30
6th move 5 to 1	6 to 9	6th move 15 to 19	30 to 25
7th move 15 to 18	9 to 5	7th move 27 to 32	25 to 22
8th move 18 to 22	17 to 14	8th move 19 to 24	20 to 27
9th move 1 to 6	5 to 1	9th move 32 to 23	White wins.
10th move 6 to 2	14 to 10		
11th move 22 to 18	1 to 5		
12th move 18 to 14	White loses.		

THE SPIRIT JEW'S-HARP.

During the Christmas holidays, when families are home for the season, and entertainments are the principal things desired in the long bright evenings, perhaps a few more tricks may not come amiss.

Among these the spirit jew's-harp will be sure to amuse and at the same time mystify both the older and younger members of the company, who will probably form the audience on these Christmas or New-year's evenings ; and will form a pleasant entertainment between the acts of a charade or the lapses in the music. Briefly described, the trick is as follows:

A jew's-harp is placed in the mouth, and played upon for awhile with the finger in the ordinary way. Gradually, however, the performer moves his hand away, but continues the motion of playing some distance from the mouth, while the instrument continues to play quite as clearly and distinctly as before. The hand may wave above the head, or in any position, to show the audience that no thread or string is connected with the tongue of the instrument, but must keep up the motion of playing as long as the sound continues to come.

Procure a jew's-harp with a very flexible tongue, and cover the end with a smooth ball of sealing-wax. Now place the instrument in your mouth with its tongue pointed inward, and if your tongue is placed against the ball of sealing-wax and suddenly pushed out, and as suddenly released, a sound will be produced much as if it was pushed out in the ordinary way with the finger.

After a time you will find it possible to produce different notes upon it, and with some practice will find it as possible to play tunes as by the common method.

It will now be seen that during the whole performance the music is elicited by the tongue, and not by the finger as at first appears; the placing the forefinger of the right hand to the mouth, and moving it as if playing in the ordinary way, is simply a little *ruse* to mislead the audience.

The performer should so stand that the light does not shine too strongly upon his face, and thus expose the absence of the tongue of the jew's-harp, and a complete mastery of the instrument in the inverted position should be acquired before one attempts the trick in public.

A NEW WAY TO KINDLE THE FIRE.

There are many ways given for producing fire, but the following is the most unique, and at the same time convenient, of all these various methods, as it consists in simply blowing the flame from the mouth, and so igniting the camp-fire or whatever else one wishes to burn.

To all appearances you fill your mouth with raw cotton, and then, taking a fan in your right hand proceed to make the fire. First a stream of blue smoke will be seen curling from your lips, and after a moment or two a bright spark will appear in the mass of cotton in the mouth. This spark is quickly followed by others until at last a clear bright flame bursts forth.

Many of the audience may not believe that it is a genuine flame, but a paper may be lighted from it and passed around the room, which will soon convince the most skeptical that it certainly is *bonâ fide* fire.

To perform this trick, procure from a chemist a piece of *amadon* or German tinder. This is an inexpensive material, brown in color, and soft and silky to the touch. Tear off a small piece—perhaps as large as a dime—and roll it in a small bit of cotton wool, having already *lighted* one end of the tinder. Place this with other cotton in your hand, and you are ready to produce all the fire your audience may demand.

First place the cotton which conceals the lighted tinder in your mouth—it will not burn you—and then some of the loose cotton you have in your hand; and remember to draw the breath in through the nostrils, but *breathe it out through* the mouth. This will fan the tinder and in a moment light the cotton in front of it, so that the smoke will begin to pass out with the breath; then the sparks will appear, and finally the flame, as described above. While placing fresh cotton in the mouth, you may take advantage of the fact that your hand is before your mouth to let some of the burnt cotton fall out. By exercising a little tact your audience may be mystified for a long time, and, in fact, will probably be unable to guess the secret at all, unless you yourself divulge it to them.

A HOME-MADE COMPASS.

Break a knitting-needle in two pieces, and magnetize one of the pieces by passing it two or three times over one of the poles of a strong magnet. Insert this piece through a small cork. Fix an ordinary needle in the end of the cork with the end projecting.

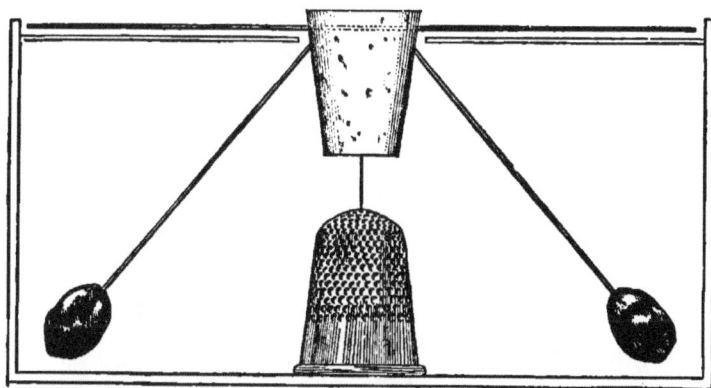

Break the other piece of the knitting-needle into two equal parts; and having wound one end of each with thread pass the other end into the cork, as seen in the illustration.

Next procure a small brass thimble, deeply indented, and balance the cork upon it by dropping melted sealing-wax upon the thread-covered ends, first on one side and then on the other, until the equilibrium is established.

A small round box is next needed, and having fitted

the top with a disk, like that seen in Fig. 2, cut the central hole large enough for the easy movement of the cork.

Now place the thimble on the bottom of the box, holding it in place with a few drops of glue. (Le Page's liquid glue is best for this, as for all occasions in which glue may be required in constructing the objects de-

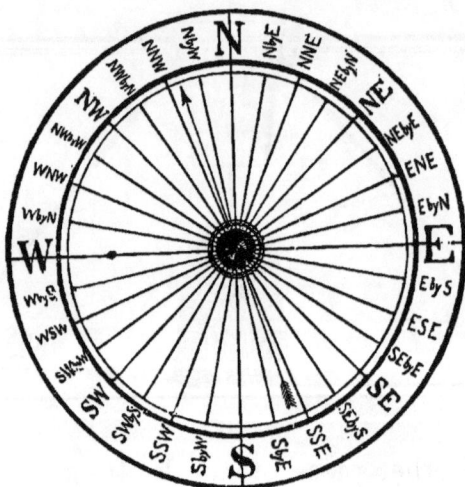

scribed in this book.) Balance the cork upon it, with the needle-point resting in one of the indentations on top of the thimble, the magnetic needle having been temporarily taken out. Now adjust the cardboard disk in place.

Lastly, insert the magnetized needle, and your compass is completed.

This compass can be made very useful upon the various

excursions into the woods which boys are always fond of taking, and, as a simple mechanical toy, much amusement may be derived from it.

By presenting the south pole of the magnet to the north pole of the compass, and jerking it quickly away, the momentum of the needle will carry it around several times before the impulse is exhausted.

The same experiment may be tried with the magnetized blade of a jackknife.

The magnetic needle does not point to the north pole of the earth, but to a point called the magnetic pole. This variation, or declination, is, from the Atlantic region of this continent, a few degrees westward of the direct north.

The arrow indicates about the average variation ; and if the compass be so placed that the needle will rest directly over it, the line N. S. will more nearly indicate the true north and south.

The card should be held in place not by glue, but by a few very short pins (filed off and re-sharpened). Then if the needle is shaken from its perch, the card can be removed to permit its re-adjustment.

HOW TO MAKE A CIRCLE.

Many of the operations described in this book require the making of circles of various sizes.

Those readers who own a pair of dividers, especially if they are furnished with a pencil-holder, will find this an easy matter. Those who are not as fortunate may be glad to learn the following ready way of describing circles accurately to any size desired.

One of the common substitutes for dividers is a loop of string or thread passed around the pencil-point, and a pin inserted in the center of the proposed circle. This is a tiresome and vexatious method, as it is difficult to tie the loop at just the right length when a circle of a specified size is to be made, the stretching of the thread adding to the perplexity. The loop is also very ready to slip up and down on the pencil or pin, making it altogether a matter of unusual good fortune to obtain a satisfactory result.

The better way is to take a strip of stout paper or thin card, about half an inch wide and a little more than half the length of the circle's diameter. A strip cut from a postal card will serve the purpose admirably.

Near one end of this make a hole large enough for the insertion of the pencil-point. Toward the other end make a pinhole, the distance of which from the first hole must be half the diameter of the circle required. Stick a pin through this hole into the center of your proposed circle ; place the pencil-point in the other, and you can achieve your result with accuracy and ease.

THE MAGNETIC CIRCUS.

This mechanical toy is comparatively simple in its construction, and will serve as the foundation for one of the many Saturday shows, which are so dearly prized by most of the bright, active boys in our land.

A good-sized soap-box serves as a table on which the toy is to rest. The back is removed, and a hole cut in the top admits the passage of the crank. It is perhaps unnecessary to add that the exposed surface of this box should be papered, or covered with a cloth curtain, in such a manner as to give it a decorative effect.

The attraction of a magnet or iron is the principle on which the "circus" is made to work.

Procure or make from thin wood a box about a foot square, and five or five and a half inches deep. Cut a hole through the central point of the bottom, to allow of the passage of the crank.

Now from a board cut a round disk which shall revolve easily inside the box, and pass through its center an axle which shall be long enough to form a support for the ring-master on the top or stage, and extend down through the top of the soap-box, where it ends in a crank by which the whole machinery is worked. On the top of this disk, and a short distance from the edge, fasten a common horseshoe magnet, which should be about four inches long, and can be bought at almost any toy store for ten cents. This must be fastened in an upright position by means of staples, as seen in the illustration.

After the magnet is arranged so that it will revolve

easily, fit the top of the box with a stiff pasteboard cover, which shall just clear the magnet; and mark upon this a circle which is to represent the ring of the circus.

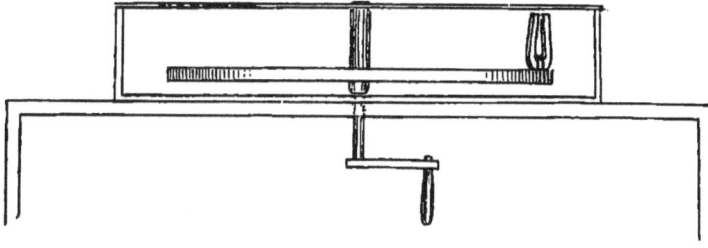

Out of stiff pasteboard cut the ring-master, and with a small nail or strong pin fix him in place. Now from four thicknesses of pasteboard cut out a horse and rider, something like that represented in Fig. 3, and insert between

the layers which form each forefoot, a nail, the head of which extends slightly below the pasteboard. File these nail-heads so that they shall be smooth and rounded.

Glue the two layers together to form the legs of the animal, and spread them slightly apart, as seen in Fig. 4 (which gives an end view of the object), having already glued all four layers to form the body of horse and rider.

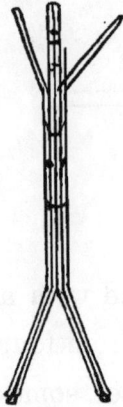

Various horses of different colors, forms, positions, and with or without riders, may be made in a similar manner; and elephants or other animals may be substituted for the horses, and made to move around the track, as if subject to the master's whip. After the glue is dry, the outside edges should be rounded and the roughnesses removed by the use of a rasp and sand-paper.

The ring-master should be so fastened, facing the horse, as to turn with each revolution of the axle.

The back of the box is fitted with a pasteboard or cloth screen, painted to represent stage scenery, and supported on either side by uprights, from the top of which float banners. For further decorations the twigs of evergreen trees are added, those of the larch or spruce, or perhaps best of all the small branches of the juniper or cedar tree, are best for the purpose. When these tiny stage trees become brown and faded, they can be easily exchanged for fresh ones, or may be painted with green paint, if a new supply is not readily obtainable.

The front of the box may be papered with fancy wall-paper, or otherwise decorated to suit the fancy of the maker; and the one who supplies the motive power, or, in other words, turns the crank, should be kept out of sight of the audience if possible. As the horses are not connected with any visible motive power, the cause of their revolution will be enveloped in a mystery which will add vastly to the entertainment of the little folks.

TO PRODUCE RAISED FIGURES ON AN EGG.

Melt some tallow, and with it paint on the shell of an egg, making letters, numbers, profiles, or any outline which your fancy may suggest, or the fineness of the brush may permit. Then immerse the egg in strong vinegar. After the lapse of a few hours, whatever is covered with the lines of tallow will project slightly, the vinegar, which is mainly acetic acid, having dissolved away the unprotected surface. By painting with a fine brush an intricate scroll or vine pattern, carrying it all around the egg, the result is very pretty, giving somewhat the effect of carved ivory.

AN ARITHMETICAL CURIOSITY.

Write the nine digits in their order, and multiply them by 9 ; the result will be composed of units, excepting the next to the last, thus :

$$
\begin{array}{r}
1\,2\,3\,4\,5\,6\,7\,8\,9 \\
9 \\
\hline
1\,1\,1\,1\,1\,1\,1\,1\,0\,1
\end{array}
$$

Multiply by 18, instead of 9, and the product will consist of 2's. By 27, and it will be 3's. In this manner all the digits may be obtained by multiplying by the multiples of 9 ; as 36, 45, 54, etc.

ONE WAY TO FIND THE NUMBER OF DAYS IN THE MONTH.

Count the knuckles of the hands, with the spaces between them; all the months with thirty-one days will fall on the knuckles, and those with less than thirty-one in the spaces. Thus, beginning with the forefinger of the left hand, July will come on the knuckle of the little finger; then beginning with August on the forefinger of the right hand, December will be reached at the knuckle of the third finger.

SOME ELECTRICAL EXPERIMENTS.

Considerable amusement may be derived from the electrical phenomena manifested by a sheet of stout brown paper, when friction is applied to it. Having warmed such a sheet, and rubbed it with the dry palm of the hand, or some woolen fabric, giving six or eight smooth, steady strokes, with considerable pressure, and all in one direction, away from the body, then place a bunch of keys in the center of the paper, and lift it by the ends ; a spark of electricity may now be taken from the keys.

If ordinary unglazed paper be immersed in a mixture of equal parts of sulphuric and nitric acids, then well washed with plenty of water and dried, it becomes extremely electric. If placed on a wooden table, or, better still, on a waxed cloth, and rubbed with the hand, it attracts feathers, pith-balls, fragments of paper, or other small light objects.

When suddenly stripped from the waxed cloth in a darkened room, the entire surface will have a luminous phosphorescent appearance. A spark can be taken from it by holding the finger about half an inch from the surface. If placed against the wall it will adhere to it and keep its place for several minutes.

This paper retains its electrical properties a long time. When weakened, it is sufficient to slightly heat it to restore all its energy.

THE ELECTROPHORUS.

This instrument, whose name, derived from the Greek, means *bearer of electricity*, consists of two parts ; first, a cake or disk of resin, or of shellac and wax, these substances being melted and poured into a tin mold ; second, a disk of brass, or sometimes of thin, well-dried wood, covered on each side with thin sheet-brass or even thick tin-foil. This should be fitted with a glass handle, to insulate it ; a stout, round bottle of moderate size will answer. The cake of resin is rubbed vigorously ; a surface of fur is the best to use for this, such as a cat-skin or

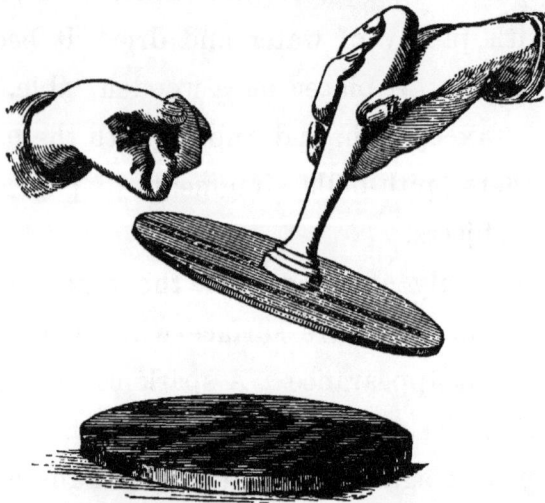

fox-tail. The disk is then taken by the handle and rested on the cake, and its upper surface touched a moment with the finger ; then, on withdrawing the disk from the resin, a bright electric spark can be obtained from it. By resting it once more on the resin, again touching and withdrawing it, another spark may be elicited, and so on for eight or ten successive trials.

The scientific explanation of this phenomenon is, that negative electricity is excited in the cake by friction. When the disk is applied, the electricity does not pass into it from the cake, but is *induced* in the disk by the law of electrical polarity; the lower surface being covered with positive electricity, while the negative is repelled to the upper side, from which it is drawn by the finger. Then, when the disk is lifted, the spark of positive electricity may be drawn.

If the construction of the instrument just described appears too formidable a task to my young readers, perhaps they may yet be inclined to experiment with

A SIMPLE ELECTROPHORUS.

Take a lacquered iron "tea-tray;" cut a sheet of stout brown paper so as to fit the flat part of the tray, and fix two strips of paper at each end by means of sealing-wax. These strips serve as handles by which to lift the paper, and the sealing-wax, being a non-conductor, prevents the electricity from passing off. The tray is also insulated by placing it upon two tumblers.

The sheet of paper is now heated quite hot, placed on a

wooden table, and rubbed with a hard and very dry clothes-brush. Then it is lifted and placed on the tray.

The paper is negatively electrified; it induces a similar state in the lower side of the tray, which should be touched a moment with the finger; then lift the paper from the tray. An electric spark can now be taken from the latter.

The strips by which the paper is lifted can be brought together, and held by the thumb and finger of one hand, leaving the other free to take the spark. The paper may now be replaced. By touching the lower surface of the tray, and lifting the paper as before, another spark may be obtained, and so on for several times, if the air be dry.

THE EBONITE ELECTROPHORUS.

This piece of apparatus, also called Pfeiffer's electrophorus, is composed of a thin sheet of ebonite, measuring about six by eight inches. A small sheet of brass, about five by three inches, is fixed on one side. With this, electricity may be evoked with unusual readiness.

It is placed flat on a wooden table, and rubbed successively on both sides with the open hand; if lifted in the left hand, and the right hand is presented to the brass, a spark will be received.

A LEYDEN JAR.

This may be made as follows : Fill a plain glass tumbler two-thirds full of shot; insert the bowl of a spoon in

the shot, leaving the handle projecting. Hold the tumbler in the hand, and bring the handle of the spoon near to the electrophorus—previously prepared for action—so as to receive its spark.   On repeating this a few times, the electric fluid will be accumulated in the "jar," and the many small sparks may be obtained as one large one, by approaching the finger to the spoon, still holding the tumbler in the other hand.

This idea may be varied by using a large wide-mouthed bottle or small jar, instead of the tumbler, and covering the outside nearly up to the top with tin-foil.   If that rare treasure, a bullet-mold, is to be had, a ball may be formed on the end of a stout wire, and used instead of the spoon, the end with the ball being the projecting one, thus making an article corresponding more nearly to the regular professional pattern.

THE PITH DANCER.

This fastidious little skipper never dances except to piano music.   It is fashioned from pith, cork, or other light material.   Generally it has a human head and body ; but when we consider its dancing extremities, we must regard it as a quadruped, or even a tripod, as the case may be; for it stands on three or four stout hog's bristles.   These may be borrowed from the floor-brush, and should be even at the lower ends, that the dancer may stand erect. It should be painted in a gay and conspicuous manner, to compensate for its diminutive size,

and a mantle of colored tissue-paper may add to its consequence. When the image is complete, stand it on the sounding-board of the piano, which should be operated with vigor. The dancer will respond to the lively notes with edifying briskness and vivacity.

THE OBEDIENT BOTTLE.

Fashion a shape like a small bottle, out of pith, paper pulp, or some other light substance. Cut a bullet in two, and fasten the base of the bottle to the flat portion of one of the halves. A straight piece of large wire, the length of the bottle, should be provided, and a hole made down through the center of the bottle, into which it will slide readily, and remain with the end out of sight. This hole

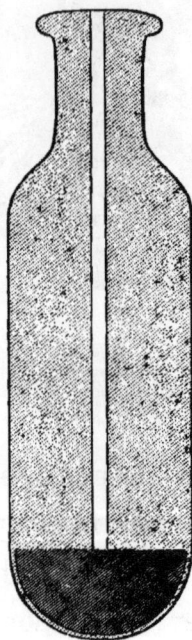

may be made with greater ease before attaching the bullet. This object can be made to yield apparent obedience to the commands of its maker. If he orders it to remain upright, he will place it on the table without inserting the wire, when nothing but constant pressure will induce it to lie prostrate. Then, taking it into his hands, and skillfully introducing the wire while the attention of the observers is directed elsewhere, he next orders it to lie flat ; and, as the weight of the wire overbalances it, it will tumble over as often as it is set up.

The bullet should be covered with thin paper as smoothly as possible, and the whole affair painted, to better conceal the *modus operandi.*

THE IMMOVABLE CARD.

If a card, such as an ordinary visiting card, is turned down about a quarter of an inch at each end, at right angles to the rest of the card, and then placed on a table so as to rest on the turned edges, you may safely challenge most persons to blow it so as to make it turn over on the other side. It would naturally seem easier to overturn a card so prepared, than one whose shape remained unchanged ; but whoever tries it will find that the facts are otherwise.

The card can be overthrown, however, by blowing on the table, toward the card, as the stream of air is then reflected against its under side.

A TRIPLE BRIDGE.

This may be constructed by means of three table-knives, in the manner illustrated in the figure. Three goblets or tumblers will serve as the piers ; these are to be arranged in a triangle, a little farther from each other than the length of the knives. Lay two of the knives on the table, with the blades crossing each other. Then pass the blade

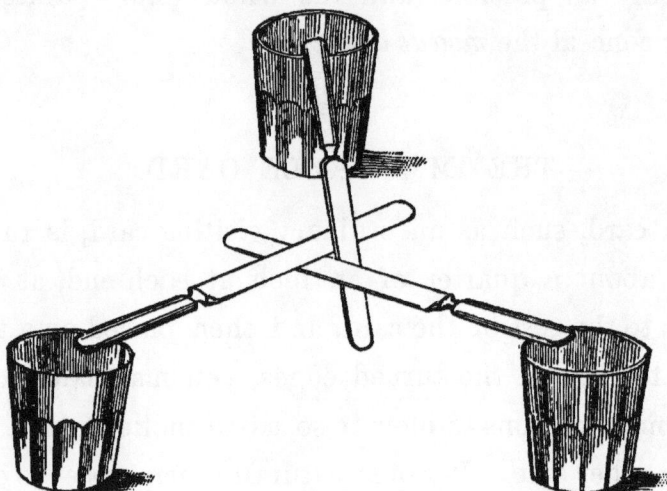

of the third knife over the uppermost blade of the other two, and under the undermost ; then take them up and place them with the ends of the handles on the rims of the glasses. The bridge now sustains itself, and if a moderate weight be placed upon it, it will be all the firmer.

AN ILLUSTRATION OF "INERTIA."

Inertia is defined as the tendency of a body to persevere in its state either of rest or motion. It is generally used in the sense of persisting in a state of rest. Among the many illustrations of this property of matter, is one which figured in the text-books of thirty or forty years ago, and which the boys of that time adapted to their amusement by constructing the apparatus here illustrated.

It consists of three parts : the board which forms the base, a post about six inches high, and a strip of stout whalebone, or dry, elastic wood.

The board should be as much as seven-eighths of an inch in thickness, and the elastic strip or spring should be firmly inserted in an inclined slit cut through the board. The places of the spring and post should be so adjusted to each other, that when the latter is secured solidly by a good-sized screw passing up through the board, the former will press with its upper end against the top of the post (as shown by the dotted line) with some degree of force.

The top of the post should be hollowed slightly, to retain the ball ; and the appearance of the whole will be improved by a coat of shellac or paint.

Now place a card on the top of the post ; and if it is sufficiently level, a marble or bullet may be induced to remain on it, directly over the column ; if not, a large bean, a spool, or a coin, will prove more tractable. Draw back the spring with the thumb and finger, as in the illustration ; let it go *suddenly*, and it will snap the card away, leaving the superimposed object resting quietly on the top of the column.

The same principle is sometimes illustrated by balancing a card on the finger, placing a coin on the card, and

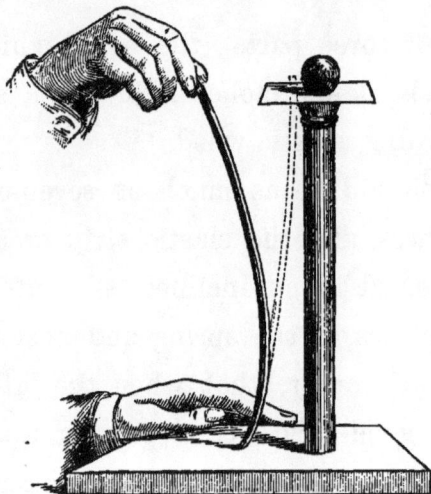

snapping away the card with the other hand, the coin remaining on the finger.

Another way is to pile up a small tower with "checkers" or "draughts." By a quick blow with a ruler, one checker may be knocked from between the others, without overturning the tower.

OTHER CHRISTMAS HOLIDAY AMUSEMENTS.

Perhaps one evening of this ever delightful season might not be more entertainingly spent than in witnessing an exhibition of some feats in *Magic*, if any lad of the company could become sufficiently expert in the art to render them with a fair amount of skill.

There are many of these mysterious tricks performed by the professional "Thaumaturgist" or "Prestidigitateur," but as most of them require a complicated or expensive apparatus, I shall only call your attention to such as are comparatively simple, and require but few "aids" or materials for their fulfillment.

HOW TO PALM A COIN.

As it is necessary for any boy or girl who intends to become an expert sleight-of-hand performer to be a successful pa'⁊ᵉr, this is naturally the first lesson to be learned. Indeed, very few of the tricks performed by an expert prestidigitateur would be effective without its use.

To explain this art is difficult, although it is an easy matter to show how the thing is done. By the aid of an illustration may be seen, however, the final position of the coin, or how it is held while it is palmed.

If possible, balance a half-dollar on the tip of the second finger of the right hand ; but if not at first easily accomplished let the coin rest on the tips of the second and third fingers, steadying it, in this position, by touching it lightly with the thumb. Close the hand quickly and the coin will rest in the palm. Then, by throwing the thumb forward, the ball of the thumb will hold the silver piece on one side, and that part of the palm which

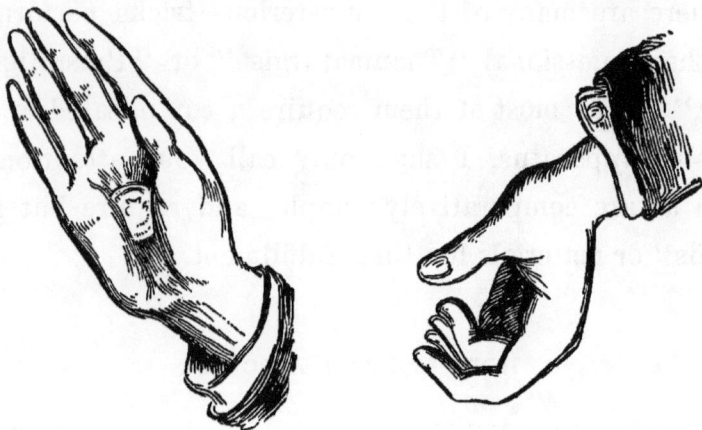

lies between the second and third fingers holds it securely on the other.

Practice this well, and be sure you can depend upon yourself to accomplish it perfectly with the left as well as the right hand, before you try any of the following tricks in the presence of a critical audience.

HOW TO PASS A COIN.

Borrow of your audience two half-dollars and lay them on your table.

Next shake your sleeves and let your friends see that you have no coins hidden about you. When they are convinced that such is the case, pick up one half-dollar with the thumb and second finger of your *right hand*. Palm this in your right hand while you *pretend* to pass it to your left, of course making a motion with the *left hand* as if it received and still held the coin.

The right hand will then *seem* to be empty, although still holding the half-dollar. Next pick up the other coin with the right hand, and place the hand behind you, being careful to keep the left well in front, and always in sight of your audience. Make some few remarks concerning the difficulty of the trick, and at last pronounce the magic word "Pass"; at the same time clink the two coins together, as if one had hit the other in the meeting. Then bring the right hand forward, and, opening it and the left at the same time, show that the coin has actually left the latter and entered the former, as you promised it should do.

HOW TO ROB PETER AND ENRICH PAUL.

Twenty pieces of money are necessary for this trick ; and two-cent pieces, or quarters, are perhaps the most convenient sizes to use. Of these, borrow fifteen from your audience, the other five have at hand, but concerning which your friends are to know nothing.

10

Having borrowed them from the company, count out five, and give them to one of your audience, while to another you give ten, and after having seen that the latter counts his carefully, take those given to the first, mutter some cabalistic nonsense, and order them to pass into the hands of the one who has the ten pieces. Finally, request him to count them again, when, strange to relate, he will find that he has fifteen, instead of the ten pieces which he was supposed to have.

The trick is performed in this manner : Upon receiving the money, throw it upon a plate or box cover—the plate is the best—and passing it to the first person, request him to take five of the pieces away. Now give the remaining money, with the plate, to the second, and ask him to drop each coin as he counts it, on the plate, that all may know he has counted correctly.

Then comes the only difficult part of the trick. Ask the one who has counted the coins to hold both his hands, while you pour the money into them, and taking the plate in your left hand, pour the contents into your right, where you have already *five more palmed* (the five the audience have not seen). Now pour the fifteen into the hands of number two, and impress upon him the importance of keeping his hands well closed over the money. This will prevent his noticing that an addition has been made. Take the five from person number one, and pretend to place them in your other hand, but instead palm them. Do your talking and command the money to pass. If you have taken proper care in palming your coins, the audience, as well as the one holding the money, will be greatly amazed by the trick.

DANGER OF REPETITION.

In almost any performance of this kind, the audience, especially if of one's intimate friends, are anxious for the performer to try again whatever strikes them as strange or mysterious, being of course on their guard to watch certain movements, at points in the performance which they had scarcely noticed before.

So it is very unsafe to try any trick over again immediately after it has been once performed, or in fact during the same evening; although perhaps it might be safely done if a number of different ones intervened. If beseeched to try it "just once more," make as graceful an excuse as you can, and suggest in its place something equally interesting.

THE INEXHAUSTIBLE HAT.

For this trick, seven half-dollars are required, and are concealed in the right hand by "palming," as the five two-cent pieces were hid in the former trick.

First, borrow of one of your audience a tall silk hat, promising to return it "as good as new" at the end of the performance.   Let the audience examine it to see that the owner is not in league with yourself, and then, walking to the back of the room, place it upon a table. While walking toward the table, with the back toward the audience, palm your coins, which should be held in some convenient pocket, readily accessible when the moment comes for using them.

Next, turn to your audience, having your coins well concealed in your right hand, and request some one to lend you *six* half-dollars; but immediately, under the pretense of disliking to trouble them, step forward, and, excusing yourself for the liberty, take a coin from the folds of a lady's dress, by simply letting one of those concealed in your hand slip to the end of your fingers. If you have had sufficient practice in "coining" you will find no difficulty in doing this, and your audience will be inclined to believe you actually found the money secreted in the fabric, although they may believe you had some hand in placing it in its hiding-place.

If you have been thus far successful, go to the hat, and, calling attention to the fact, drop the half-dollar into it ; then, as if you imagined some one was doubtful whether the coin was really in the hat, make some remark to the effect that if they do not believe you dropped it you will do so again, at the same moment thrusting your hand down to the crown to take it in sight again.

At the moment the hand is in this position, carefully place the six half-dollars on the bottom, and let one remain in the palm. Pick up one of these six, and holding it high, let it drop, being careful, however, that it does not hit the other five.

The coin in your hand you proceed to take from any unusual place which may occur to you—the window curtain, portière, a gentleman's beard, or a lady's coiffure, are those most naturally suggested. As soon as you take a half-dollar from its hiding-place, you pretend to place it in your left hand, and from there command it to pass to the hat, but in reality you palm it in your right where it is ready for the next position from which you desire to take it. Proceed in this way until you have gathered in six half-dollars.

As these have been lying quietly in the hat during all this time, you have no anxiety about sending them there, and must simply avoid going near it while apparently filling it with the money. When the last silver piece has been sent to its destination, request the audience to select some one of its members to count the money in the hat, and see that none has been lost in its flight hence. It will, of course, be found all right, and great will be the curiosity to know how you placed it there; but do not allow yourself to be influenced into trying it a second time, for with the close watching you will undergo your secret will be discovered.

ANOTHER HAT TRICK.

The hat may well be called "inexhaustible," for all manner of things may be made to come from its prolific crown, and in such profusion, that a receptacle of double its size would hardly contain them.

If two boys have learned the art of palming well, they may assist each other, and, if at all ingenious, invent a variety of tricks for an evening's amusement.

The following is but a suggestion, which may be varied by different materials :

Let them borrow from the audience two tall silk hats, and place them upon chairs standing some distance from each other. Each having provided himself with a small rubber ball—the one resembling the other as nearly as possible—they are ready to proceed.   The hats were of course empty when passed to the stage, but as the first boy takes his place, back of the chair which contains a hat, he should glance down into it, and with surprise, draw out a ball which he has had concealed in his right hand, show it to the audience and then pretend to put it in his left hand, but instead *palm* it in the right; at the same time extending his left toward his partner.   The second boy stretches out his right arm as if to receive the ball, and at the moment his hand touches the fingers of No. 1, he lets that which he has been palming in his right hand slip down to his fingers, as if he had just received it from his friend. Now, pretending to change it to his left, he palms it, as No. 1 has done, and finally drops his left hand, which is supposed to hold the ball, into the hat in front of him, at the same time giving the side or crown a rap with one of his fingers, to imitate the falling of the ball. This same thing may be repeated indefinitely, until you have balls enough to stock the village. When you see the audience is beginning to tire, let No. 1 say, " My hat is empty ; shall I help you count the balls in yours ?" No. 2 nods assent, and looks down, as if expecting the hat to be full. He must then pretend great surprise, and taking up the hat must turn it upside down, gently shake it—remembering it is borrowed—and with the audience wonder what has become of all the balls.

Eggs, small lemons or oranges, little china dolls, and a number of small toys may be substituted for the rubber balls above given.

THE PERAMBULATING EGG.

This trick is one of the easiest, while at the same time one of the most pleasing, of the magician's arts. In it an egg, apparently without any impulse beyond that which resides within itself, travels over a hat, and after reconnoitering it in its every nook and corner, passes gracefully over to another, and commences its journey of discovery around the second in much the same manner it has traversed the first.

Two hats are borrowed from the audience, and a dish of eggs is placed upon the table by their side, when the performer requests the lady stationed at the piano to give some music, and the exhibition commences. The egg which is used is merely a shell, the inside having been sucked or blown out through tiny holes made at either end. A slender silken thread is tied to the upper button of the performer's waistcoat, while attached to the other end is a small piece of wax or other sticky substance. Just before the performance commences, show the dish of eggs, and then pass away from them and back of your audience, to show that they (the eggs) are in no way attached to your person.

As the music strikes up, walk to the table, take the shell from the dish, making it appear that you had no choice, but took the first one you chanced to touch, and place it inside the hat, at the same moment pressing the bit of wax to its side.

As the egg is *in the hat* it is necessary for it to pass out upon the outside surface. To do this the hat is slowly moved downward until the egg is even with the brim;

then by careful management and a little practice, the effect is produced of the egg walking up the hat instead of the hat being lowered to the egg. You may now take the egg in your hand and, holding the hat with the crown upward in a horizontal position, place it beneath the egg, and turn it slowly away from yourself. The effect will be that the egg is traveling up hill. By placing the other hat close to the one upon which you are performing, and slowly drawing it under the egg, the latter will appear to pass over to the crown of the second hat, and very much the same movements may be repeated on this as on the first.

THE MAGIC DISPATCHER.

Borrow a quarter or half-dollar from your audience, and ask the owner to place some mark upon it by which it may be identified. Wrap this in the corner of a hand-kerchief, and give it to some one to hold. Next take a ball of yarn, and having placed it in a tumbler, ask some other person in your audience to hold his hand over the top of the tumbler in such a way that the ball will be kept in place, and the yarn will run smoothly through the fingers. Hold one end of the yarn some distance from the tumbler, or near where the coin is held, and inform your audience that, as your dispatcher is in good working order, you will proceed to send the coin your friend has in his hand into the very center of the ball of yarn. Take the opposite corner of the handkerchief from the one holding the money in your right hand, and having counted one, two, three, command the coin to pass, at the same instant snatching the handkerchief from your

friend's hand. Next commence to unwind the ball, being careful to keep some distance from the tumbler while so doing.

As the yarn is nearing its end, the silver piece will drop upon the bottom of the tumbler, and nothing is left for you to do but to request the owner of it to step forward and see if it is the one he lent you.

In this, as in many of the tricks you have already learned, very little preparation is required. First, a coin of the same denomination as the one borrowed is sewed in a corner of the handkerchief. The ball is wound upon a stick of a particular shape, which is drawn out when the coin is to be substituted in its place. This stick should be about two and a half inches long, one and a quarter inches wide, and an eighth of an inch thick, rounded off at one end, and scraped until it is perfectly smooth.

When winding your ball, be careful to have the rounded end of the stick in the center of the ball, and the other end projecting slightly on one side.

After you have procured your coin, palmed it, and given the handkerchief containing the other into the hands of some person to hold, go for your ball, which should be at some distance from your audience, that you may have time to draw out the stick and insert the coin in its place, while you are walking back to the table upon which is your tumbler.

The trick is now done, but the audience must be kept ignorant of the fact, while your conversation and subsequent acting should shroud it in all the mystery possible.

THE TURKISH RING TRICK.

A few years ago I had the good fortune to see a famous magician perform. Many and wonderful were the things he did, and at times it seemed as if other than human skill must be aiding him in his craft.

Among others, he gave the following trick, which was as enthusiastically applauded as many of the others. It had for me no element of strangeness, as I was already initiated into its secret. Since it has ever been a favorite in the little amateur performances we have from time to time been in the habit of giving, I hope it may gain a wider popularity in the larger circle of friends to whom I am about to disclose it.

To the public it appears as follows: A plain gold ring is borrowed, placed in a handkerchief, and given to a person to hold. A small stick is held by two others, in such a position that its center is hidden by the handker-

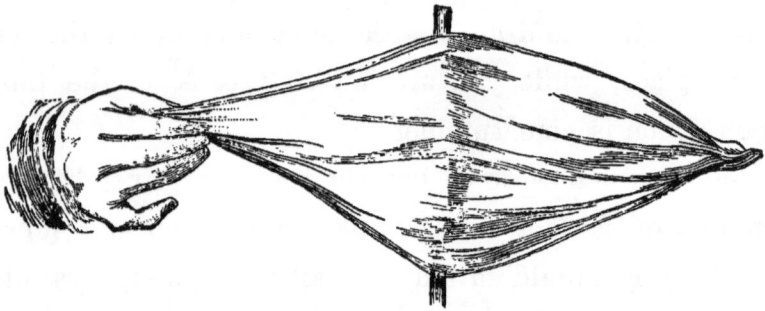

chief; each person holds an end. The magician commands the ring to pass, at the same moment snatching the handkerchief, a corner of which he has taken, away from the one holding it—when behold ! the ring, which a moment ago was in the spectator's hand, is now whirling around the stick, which it evidently has just reached.

It is performed as follows: When the ring is taken from its owner, it is palmed, and not placed in the handkerchief, as one is led to suppose, the handkerchief being supplied, as you probably have already guessed, with a ring which is sewed in its end. In passing the stick to the holders, you have simply to pass it through the right hand, in the center of which your ring is palmed, and, of course, through the ring itself. Then, holding it until it is hidden by the handkerchief, is not difficult to do. When you first take up the stick, be sure and use your left hand, so that you will have it ready to pass through your ring without any awkward or suspicious movements. Finally, pulling the handkerchief suddenly and quickly across the stick, causes the ring to whirl upon it very much as if it had just dropped in its place. It is always well, when performing with the handkerchief, to have a second and similar one in your pocket, to show in case suspicion should be aroused concerning it.

HOW TO MELT AND RE-COIN A HALF-DOLLAR.

Supply your table with a candle in a light candlestick, and a glass of water. When ready to perform, request some one of your audience to lend you a half-dollar, suggesting at the same time, that a new bright coin would best suit your purpose.   Have it marked that the owner may be sure of its identity.

If nothing but dull coins are to be found, have a small bottle of ammonia at hand, and holding the piece in your hand, pour a few drops of the liquid upon it ; let it stand a few moments and then wipe with a bit of cloth.   Treat both sides in the same way, and brighten up the edges in like manner.   All this while you may be talking of this treatment, as if it were intended to render the metal more fusible, but be careful not to mention what the fluid is, or for what it is really intended.   This treatment is, of course, not necessary in the case of new coins, in which case it can be omitted.

When the silver is bright, and presents the appearance of a new coin, take it between the thumb and forefinger of your right hand, look at it carefully, and then pretend to drop it into your left hand, but instead palm it in your right.

Now continue to move your left hand as if working the coin around in it, keeping up a continual flow of small talk during the whole performance.   The difficulty of melting silver, the amount of heat required, and the comparative hardness of different metals, forming good subjects, with which you will become familiar before your public exhibition.

To render the idea of palming an apparent impossibility, take up the candle in your right hand. This will render the holding of the coin less troublesome, and appear to your audience as a conclusive evidence that the half-dollar is in your left hand.

After you have pretended to place the coin in your left hand, do not for an instant forget to appear as if it really was there, and keep that hand always in sight of your audience.

Having taken the lighted candle in your right, hold the left hand above the flame, and move the fingers as if allowing the silver to pass down, drop by drop, into the candle itself. If, just before this, previous to taking the candle, you could catch up the glass for a drink and drop a spoonful of water into the hollow of your left hand, the dropping of it into the candle-flame would add to the impression of melting silver. You can wet your hand slightly in many natural ways, as no one would imagine the water had anything to do with the trick. Continue to pretend to drop the silver, until it would naturally be gone ; then, without removing your hand, open it and announce that the half-dollar is melted, and can be found in the candlestick ; assuring the donor that he need not be alarmed, as you can bring it out as it was before it went in, if he will but have patience.

Put the candlestick down upon the table, and pretend to pick out bits of silver from the various parts of it with the right hand, placing them as they are gathered in the palm of the left hand. At a convenient moment, when the right is exactly above the left hand, drop the half-dollar into it, and the trick is done. But it would not do to let the audience know this, so you must continue to work the left hand as if molding the coin in shape, blowing with the mouth into the palm as if cooling the heated mass ; toss it from hand to hand as if to cool it more rapidly, and finally return it to the spectator from whom it was borrowed.

BURNING THE CENTER FROM A HANDKERCHIEF.

The young performer will find but little difficulty in performing this simple sleight-of-hand trick successfully. A lighted candle, a small stick, or magic wand, and a piece of thin cambric or muslin about six inches square, are the materials required.

Place the lighted candle on your table, and the wand on another table or shelf some distance from the former with the bit of cambric behind it.

Now borrow of some lady present a handkerchief, a gentleman's being inconveniently large. Take the handkerchief by the center, pull it carefully between the fingers and thumb of left hand, and advance toward the candle.

Just as you are about to burn it, stop and say, as if in

answer to some remark overheard, "Oh, no, I have not changed the handkerchief. See!" and at the same time allow another inspection of it.

Suggest now to its owner, if, in case her handkerchief is burned, she would like it restored again to its proper condition; and, upon her answering in the affirmative, announce the necessity of the magic wand for that purpose. Walk to the spot where the wand is lying, and take it up, managing to pick up at the same time between the left thumb and forefinger the bit of cambric; the center of this piece should be pointed outward so that it may be readily pulled out at the desired moment, the remainder being neatly rolled up and palmed under the thumb. This piece should have been rolled up with the central point slightly projecting when first placed on the shelf, and the performer should manage to turn his back toward the audience for a few moments when taking up the wand.

Place the wand in one of your coat pockets as you advance toward your candle, and again take the handkerchief, putting it this time into the left hand, and pull up the small piece of material, completely hiding the center of the real handkerchief between the second and third fingers and the palm of the hand.

The portion of the cambric extending beyond the thumb and forefinger may now be safely burned, and

the audience may be sure the handkerchief is burned, as
you can make some display of rolling it up in a ball, taking care, however, to separate the burned piece from the
real article. Now take the wand from the pocket, and
at the same time manage to drop the small semi-burned
piece of muslin unperceived into the pocket; touch the
handkerchief with the wand, and, after some magic word
or words, return the handkerchief to the owner to be examined, remarking that you hope not even an odor of
smoke is noticeable about it.

Whenever displaying feats in magic, it is better for the
performer to go forward among the audience if he has
anything to show or have examined, than to allow the
latter to come to his portion of the room. His table has
often some things upon it which if seen near by would
do much toward dispelling the mystery connected with
his works.

A wide space should be left between his table and the
front row of spectators, as he often has occasion to step
between the two in some of his feats.

The lights also should be judiciously arranged, so as
not to shine too directly upon his hands or person, or
even upon his table. Always have everything you can
possibly need in some easily accessible place, and in just
the position most convenient to be taken.

Decide beforehand what tricks you will perform, and

in just what order they are to be given. Of course, all the materials are not to be spread on the table at the commencement of the entertainment, as they would be in the way, and confuse you in your first acts ; but they should all be at hand, and while articles are being examined which have passed through the various vicissitudes in a former trick, you can utilize the time when the attention is thus carried away from yourself to gather together and properly place the materials for your next feat.

Never be induced to perform a trick a second time, unless nearly a whole evening's performance intervenes. Even then it is pretty sure to be detected.

THE MAGIC ROPE.

Take a piece of clothes-line, six or seven yards long, and pass it among your audience for inspection. While it is going its rounds, have your hands securely tied with a handkerchief, which should be passed around the wrists and knotted on one side.

When the rope is returned to you, drop one end between your arms, or inside the handkerchief, and request some one to take both ends of the rope and pull, to make sure your hands are firmly tied. It would now seem impossible to get the rope off, unless the hands were untied or the ends released. After two or three rapid motions, however, the rope drops to the floor, while your hands remain tied as at first.

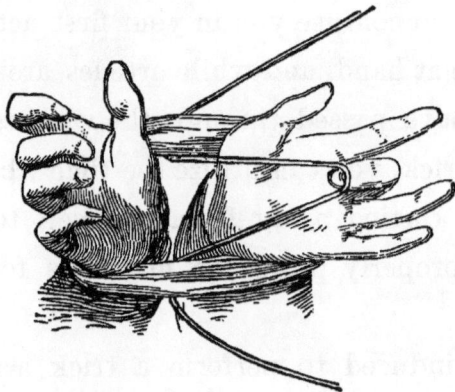

First, do not have your hands tied so tightly that you cannot move them ; this can be arranged by holding them slightly apart while they are being tied. After the rope has been pulled by the holder, it is somewhat relaxed ; and then, by rubbing it between the wrists a loop may be formed, into which the second finger may be slipped. The whole hand is now readily thrust through, and only a jerk is necessary to send the rope upon the floor. In performing this trick, work as quickly as possible, that your movements may not be easily followed.

A CAMPING-OUT COOKING-STOVE.

Although the winter season is now well upon us, and its reigning king, Jack Frost, jealous if we but mention the "camp-fire," has covered its very site with ice and snow, we need not fear incurring his displeasure by the following exhibition.

Procure an old silk hat if possible, and pass it among your audience for inspection. Have upon the stage, or at your end of the room, a table, with a drawer open at the back. In this drawer have a small cake in the tin in which it was baked. Let it be made in a patty-pan if convenient. Beside this cake have a small tin cup, which will fit rather tightly into the mouth of a china jar you have also provided. On the top of the table have an unlighted candle, the jar, which should be porcelain if possible, a basket containing a few eggs, a pitcher of water, some flour, and a box marked sugar. The hat, after having been examined, is returned to you; and the cake, along with the cup which is to receive the eggs and flour, are put into it. This is effected as follows: Take the cake and cup in your left hand, keeping it down behind the table, and your hat in the right hand; bring the cake and cup up to the edge, and immediately cover it with the hat, which you begin brushing with your right. Keep up a running discourse all the time, so that the movement will seem natural, and not be suspected. In a moment or two partly withdraw the left hand, and grasping the brim of the hat, turn it upside down upon the table. If the tin is not in a good position to catch the eggs and flour which you are to drop into it, palm a penny and pretend to find it in the hat, chiding your audience for carelessly over-looking it, remarking that although a useful thing to have, it is not exactly a proper ingredient for cake. Of course, while pretending to pick up the coin, you can ar-range the tin cup on top of your cake in the middle of the hat. Be sure that it stands firm.

Now proceed to break one or more eggs, and drop the contents into the hat, taking especial care that they drop into the cup. Next throw in a spoonful of sugar, and then pour a few drops of water and one or two spoonfuls of flour into the jar, and stir well with a spoon. Pour the contents of the jar into the cup, and then, under pretense of draining the last drop into the hat, force the jar down over the cup, and work it around until the cup is well pushed up into the mouth of the jar. It is needless to add that you must pretend all the while that you are scraping or shaking out the mixture. The jar can now be taken out and carelessly placed behind the sugar-pail or any other object, to prevent the edge of the tin cup from being seen.

The trick is now completed, the only necessary thing to do is to keep up the acting until the cake is supposed to be finished.

First, stir it well by moving the spoon around quite actively in the hat; then light the candle, and, informing your audience that the cake is ready for baking, take the hat in one hand and hold it over the candle for a minute or two, occasionally glancing in to see if it is doing well.

In a short time announce that it is baked ; and after blowing out the candle, take the cake from the hat, turn it out upon a plate, and placing a knife by its side, pass it to some one to cut, and politely request your friends to try it, and judge upon the efficacy of your camp-stove. If the hat was borrowed, return it with thanks to its owner, and congratulate him upon having such a useful article always on hand.

NECESSITY OF A SOBER COUNTENANCE.

In most, in fact all, of these exhibitions, it is absolutely necessary that one should keep a sober countenance while performing. No matter how hard your audience laugh, do not allow the shadow of a smile to flit across your face. If you do it will take away much of the effectiveness and half the mystery, from whatever you are doing.

I once had a young friend, a quick bright boy, who was very successful in palming, and in many of the other elements in sleight-of-hand tricks, but he had a ridiculous and unconquerable habit of laughing whenever his audience laughed, and, in fact, of sometimes anticipating the laugh, and commencing before his friends saw anything worth laughing about.

He was of course not successful, and was never watched with as much interest as his brother, who, although not as clever, was as sober as a judge from the beginning to the end of the performance. No amount of hilarity in the audience affected him in the least. If he found it was impossible to make himself heard, he stood still and waited; but always with the same quiet, calm countenance he would have worn had he been walking up the aisle of a church. Learn to command your countenance, as one of the most important requisites of a successful magician.

THE GREAT CHINESE ROPE FEAT.

Many years ago this trick was exhibited in a show-window on Broadway, but as probably most of the people who then saw it have long since forgotten how it was performed, I give the following account:

Two ropes, each about three yards in length, are given to the audience to examine, which of course are pronounced perfect; then they are passed through the sleeves of a coat, in such a way as to suspend it; the ends are then given to two boys to hold. The performer then places his hand inside the coat, and having requested those who are holding the ends of the rope to pull, the coat falls to the floor, having in some mysterious manner worked off the ropes.

Of course, the whole secret of this trick depends upon the arrangement of the ropes, which are of themselves perfect. After they have been examined, and are returned to the performer, he pretends to measure them, and while so doing manages to bend each rope double;

A ——————————————————————————— B

that is, he brings the two ends of each together; while still holding them he contrives to slip a small elastic band over the center of one, and bringing the middle of the other alongside of it, he slips the band over both, thus tying them together, as shown in the illustration.

Now holding this juncture carelessly in his left hand, over which arm a coil or two of the rope is thrown, he passes the ends marked *A* through one sleeve of the coat,

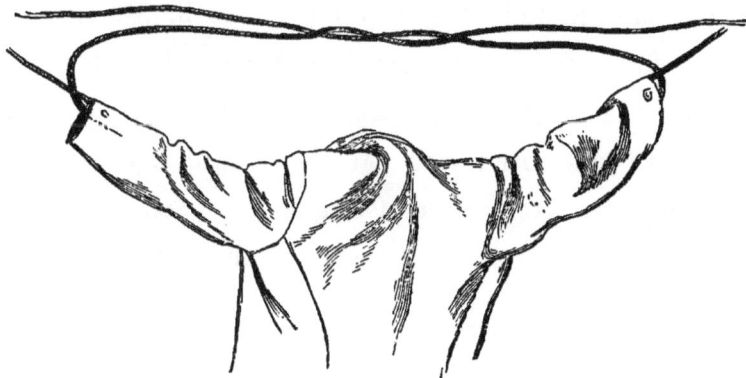

and the end marked *B* through the other, and these are the ends he gives to the two persons to hold.

If he now slips off the rubber band, the coat will fall ; but each person will have both ends of the same rope in his hand, and the mystery would be easily solved. To remedy this, however, the performer, under pretense of making the trick still more difficult, takes an end from each of the holders, and proceeds to tie a single loop, as seen in the illustration, thus reversing the ends, which he then returns to them.

Of course, when the band is taken off, each person has but one end of either rope in his hand.

TO PULL A STRING THROUGH A BUTTON-HOLE.

Tie together the ends of a piece of string about two feet long ; pass it thus tied through a button-hole of your coat. Hitch the two ends on your thumbs, and catch up with each little finger the upper string on the thumb of the opposite hand ; then, stretching the hands apart, the string will appear in a very complicated tangle. If the hold of the right thumb and left little finger, or *vice versâ*, be then loosed, and the hands quickly separated, the string will come away from, and appear as if it had passed through, the outside edge of the button-hole.

TO UNITE A PARTED STRING.

Take a piece of string about four feet long ; hold the ends, pointed upward, between the first and second finger and thumb of the left hand, and the first finger and thumb of the right hand, letting the remainder of the string hang down in a loop. Now bring the right hand close to the left, crossing at right angles that end of the cord held in the left hand, and continue to pull until half the length of the string has passed the left hand, at the same time slipping the third finger of the left hand between the two parts of the string.

The first finger and thumb of the right hand should then seize the string at a point just below the little finger of the left hand, the third finger of that hand at the same time drawing back the string toward the palm of the hand.

The part of the string now held horizontally between the two hands is only the continuation of the end held in the left hand, though it will appear to be the middle of the string.

This piece of the string some one of the audience should be invited to cut, and thus apparently divide the string in halves, although in fact he only cuts off two or three inches.

Place all the ends of the string between the teeth, withdraw the short piece with the tongue, and show the remainder, apparently as the string was at the commencement.

Of course, the string must not be measured, or the trick will be detected.

A MINERAL GARDEN.

Fill a clear glass jar—a fruit jar will answer the purpose—with sand, to the depth of two or three inches; insert a few pieces of sulphate of iron, sulphate of copper, and sulphate of aluminum, so that they will be barely covered with the sand.

Now fill the jar to within about three inches of the top with a solution of silicate of soda, commonly known as "water-glass," which can be procured at most large city drug stores. This should be diluted with three times its bulk of water before it is poured in; and care should be taken not to stir up the sand and disarrange the chemicals.

After standing about a week, the silicates of the various bases will appear in a luxuriant and variously colored growth, resembling vegetation.

Now the silicate solution may be displaced with clear water, which should be poured in very carefully, so as not to break or disturb the vegetation. This permanent miniature forest will be found to present a very attractive appearance, and as no pruning or weeding are required, the young gardener will probably feel that his trouble is well repaid. Its development from day to day will be watched with interest by all the members of the household, although it will be of especial value to the invalid, to whom any new and interesting object to watch is a blessing indeed.

Another pleasing and ingenious device I insert for the benefit of this class of my readers, wishing, in the meantime, that it might be in my power to make their in-door life so bright and full of interest, that they would forget the more active sports of their sturdy brothers and sisters, or at least cease to regret their enforced confinement. This little affair I shall call

THE CRYSTAL VASE.

This sparkling ornament will almost make itself, so little trouble is required.

You have only to half fill a tall glass tumbler with water, and put in half a teacupful of table salt, then let it stand.

As the water dries out, put in a little more, adding salt also in due proportion ; and keep this up for five or six months.

By degrees an incrustation of crystals will fill the tumbler, and spread gradually down the outside; extending and thickening till the whole vessel is covered with an irregular glittering mass, which might well be the work of the ice-sprites in the kingdom of Jack Frost.

As the crystals approach the bottom of the tumbler, the

latter should be set in a saucer ; when the tiny stalactites have enveloped this also, the vase is complete.

Should it be desired to enhance still further the decorative effect of this by the use of color, a blue tint can be communicated by adding a little indigo blueing to the salt and water. Should other colors be desired, almost all of those employed in coloring alum crystals (see page 25) may be used with equal success in this case. By adding different colors at different times, a variegated effect may be produced.

The gradual growth of the crystals, and enlargement of the mass, is a very interesting spectacle.

THREE CHRISTMAS OR BIRTHDAY GIFTS.

When speaking of Christmas presents in an earlier portion of this book, I unintentionally omitted three quite interesting and easily made puzzles, which are always pleasing sources of amusement to the young folks, and sure to while away many half-hours on stormy days. Such presents are always valuable additions to the nursery closet, and in an indirect way are as gratifying to mamma and nurse as to the little recipient himself. The first of these is called the

OCTAGON PUZZLE.

This puzzle consists of twelve irregular pieces of stiff

pasteboard or wood, which are to be arranged in the form of an octagon.

Although these pieces can be cut from pasteboard, they are more lasting, stronger, and better every way if made of wood. White holly, such as is employed for brackets, is a nice material to use.

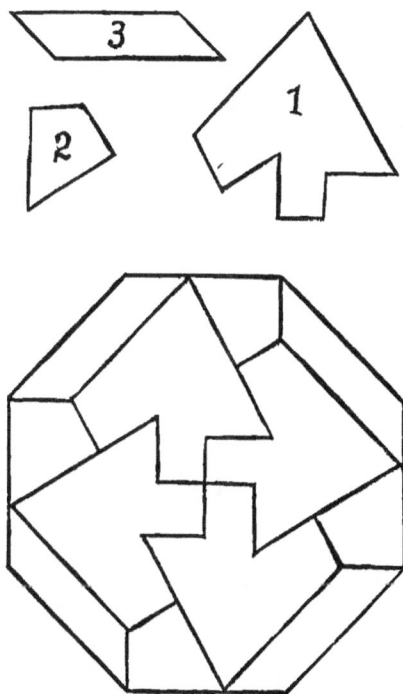

With a jig-saw cut four pieces in shape like that represented in Fig. 1, four like Fig. 2, and four more like Fig. 3; rub the edges down with sand-paper, and, if you like, paint each set a different color. When the paint is dry, varnish them.

Pack them in a small pasteboard box, which you can neatly cover with paper—any fancy color will do—and you will find your little brother or sister will be as well pleased with them as with many toys which have come direct from the store.

Another puzzle of the same character as this is

THE CROSS PUZZLE.

In this, as in the Octagon, the pieces composing the cross may be made of pasteboard, but are better and

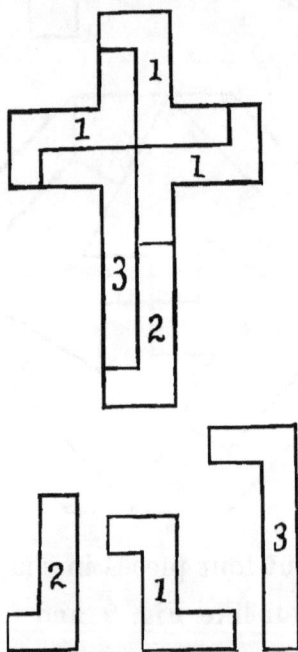

stronger if made of the white holly or other thin "bracket wood."

Cut three pieces—with the jig-saw, of course—in shape like Fig. 1, one piece like Fig. 2, and one like Fig. 3.

These pieces may be of any size, but relatively each one must correspond with the sizes and shapes indicated in the diagram.

Paint as fancy may dictate, after smoothing the edges off with sand-paper. Pack in a box treated like that used for the "Octagon Puzzle."

The last of these interesting puzzles is known as the

SQUARE PUZZLE.

Of the pasteboard or white holly cut out eight squares of whatever size desired ; divide four of them into halves by cutting them from corner to corner, so there are in all twelve pieces.

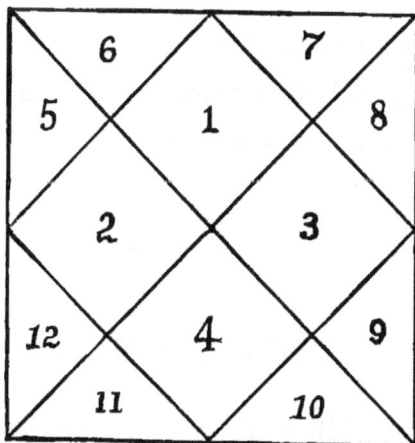

The puzzle is to form a square of these twelve pieces. The illustration shows how this is done.

11

When these puzzles are given to the little folks, no "key" should accompany them, but the children should try to put them together without help. If, however, you find they begin to lose interest, show them the first step, and encourage them to try to finish it by themselves.

There are great differences in children in this respect ; some persevering and unwilling to be helped at all, while others become discouraged at the smallest obstacles and refuse to try. The latter should be encouraged by a little help, care being taken, however, that they do a considerable portion of the work themselves.

No doubt this "indolence," as it is sometimes erroneously called, is generally due to a weak physical condition, rather than to inferior mental powers. A child of this temperament, instead of being ridiculed by his more vigorous companions, should be encouraged and stimulated to action ; and such games or puzzles as those contained in this book are just the things to accomplish this end.

A SIMPLE FOUNTAIN.

Take a bottle holding eight or ten ounces, and insert a tube in the cork. A fine glass tube or even a pipe-stem will answer.

The tube should reach nearly but not quite to the bottom of the bottle, and should fit air-tight in the cork.

Fill the bottle about three-fourths full of water, and blow with considerable force down the tube. Upon removing the mouth, the water will spurt out, forming a miniature fountain; which will continue to play as long as any water remains in the bottle.

THE FAN FROM NAGASAKI.

A few months ago, a friend who had been for several years a resident of Japan, came home to America for a visit, and brought with her a bright little son and daughter, neither of whom had ever set foot on our American shores before. The children were delighted with their American cousins; and evidently could not find words strong enough to sound the praises of the new games and sports which they were constantly learning.

Their lives had been spent with Chinese or Japanese nurses; and although kind-hearted and devoted as my friend assured me these people were, the little exiles must have had a sorry time of it in their foreign play-room, when compared with our own boys and girls. The respect and almost reverence with which they regarded Jack, the most daring scapegrace in our family, would have been very amusing had it not been pathetic. What Jack did was always marvelous in their eyes, and into many an unsuspected trap they were beguiled by his mischievous pranks. They were what most of you boys and girls would call very green, when they first reached us, but under Jack's tuition, I fear that next winter—in fact, at the very time you are reading this—perhaps they will be trying the same tricks upon their innocent Japanese nurse that Jack tried upon them.

It will not be strange if that long-suffering personage does not in his secret heart have less respect for this illustrious nation than he has been wont to have before.

But if so ignorant in most things, these children were very ingenious and uncommonly happy in making things of paper.

One rainy morning, about a week after they came to us, I had occasion to go into the nursery for something, and was quite surprised to find the children busily engaged in folding paper. Edith had brought down some rice-paper from her trunk, and with the help of her brother, was fashioning all sorts of odd things from it; while the younger members of my own family were looking on with intense interest.

I left the room, after watching them for a few minutes, but an hour later, upon entering it again, found them still employed in the same amusement.

It seems that their nurse had been in the habit of teaching them many Japanese arts to keep them still while under his charge. Their nurse was a man, strange to say, as very few female servants are employed in either China or Japan, and now they in their turn were teaching these to us. I confess the graceful, pretty things they were making had quite a fascination for me, and I even left off what I had been doing, and became a pupil with the youngsters. I took up the article which they were just beginning to learn, and, following my little teacher's directions, I made what I have styled ''The Fan from Nagasaki,'' because my little instructress was born and lived in that city, and learned her art from a native Jap, and not because the fan itself, if it can strictly be called a fan, came from that region.

The children called it by a delightfully odd Japanese name, which you would find it hard to pronounce even if I should invent a way of spelling it.

Edith used Japanese or rice paper for those she made ; but we found a stout quality of brown wrapping-paper, not too stiff, answers nearly as well.

If brown paper is used, a rectangular piece about two feet long, by one and a half feet wide, is a good-shaped piece to use.

Mark off each of the edges which measure eighteen inches into six equal parts, each division being of course

three inches long (see Fig. 1). Now double the paper on
the line at *x*, and you have a shape like Fig. 2. Fold the
uppermost half under at the line *a a*, and again outward
at the line *b b;* then fold the under half in precisely the
same manner, and your paper is like Fig. 3.

Upon examining the edge *a a a*, two openings between
the folds will be seen; whereas at the edge *b b b*, three
openings will be found. The hand has next to be placed

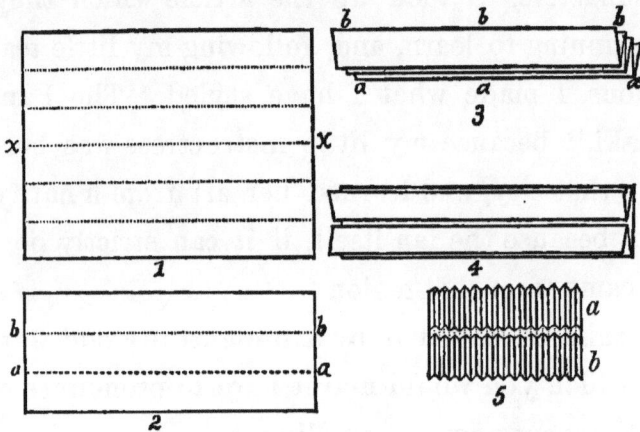

in the middle of these three openings, and the paper
spread out toward the right and toward the left; that
middle fold lying flat or unfolded for the time being.
Another figure is now made like Fig. 4. Now commencing at one end of this long strip, crinkle it the whole
length as you would a lamplighter top, making the
folds even, about a quarter or half an inch wide. Be
careful not to make these folds wider than this, as the

fan does not work as well when they are wide. You have
now a figure like that seen in Fig. 5 ; and if your folds
have been carefully and firmly creased, your paper is prepared to make all sorts of strange shapes. I think Edith
told me her nurse could make sixty-five different forms
from a similarly folded bit, and most of these she was
able to reproduce ; but as it is some time since the children left us to visit other friends, and I have not given
the subject a second thought till now, I find I have forgotten how many of the more intricate ones were formed.
Perhaps with the directions for these my readers will
catch the *knack*, as we Yankees call it, and can improvise
some forms unlike any of these, for themselves. Whatever you succeed in making, you may be quite certain
that the Nagasakian nurse, away off on the other side of
the earth, is ahead of you, and has made the same form
before ; for his sixty-five must include about everything
one could possibly fashion from its folds.

In Fig. 6, the lower edge of Fig. 5 is held between the
thumb and forefinger of the left hand, while the top is
spread out like a fan. For Fig. 7, take Fig. 6, insert the
fingers at *a*, and pass them round to *b*, raising the paper
outward. Fig. 8 is a continuation of 6 and 7, as the
upper layer of the overhanging edge in Fig. 7 is raised by
passing the finger under it at *c*, and bringing it out at *d*.

Fig. 9 is a reverse of Fig. 8. Catch the paper by the

part now uppermost, pinch that part well together, and loosen the part which was confined in Fig. 8.

It must be remembered that every time the fan is changed, the paper must be pinched into its original form, Fig. 5. It will now be necessary to make that change. After creasing the folds firmly in place (Fig. 5), lift up the upper part *a*, bring the lower plaits *b* well

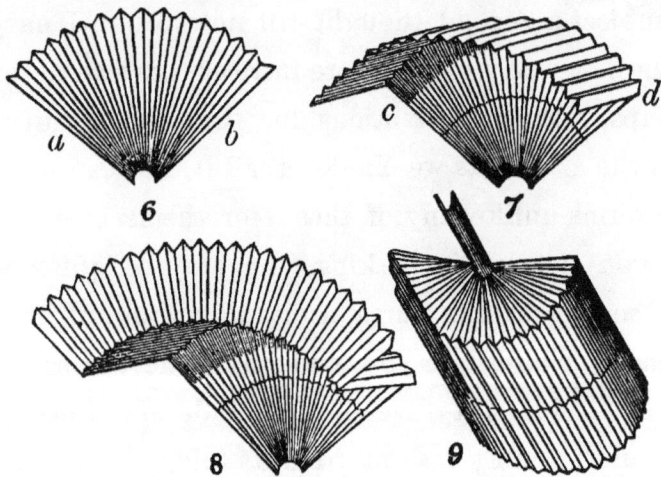

together, and hold them for the handle. With the disengaged hand, arrange the upper part in the form of a sunshade. Another form may be got by raising the upper layer of the sunshade cover, a species of cup or goblet. By drawing out *b* until it is at right angles with the upright, the goblet form is nearer correct.

Now reverse the paper, and spread out the lower part

so that it may represent the body of a wine-glass ; that which in Fig. 10 was the top of the sunshade, is now the foot of the glass, as seen in Fig. 11.

The Chinese lantern (Fig. 12) is as easily made. Open out all the paper, and twist it around ; catch it now by

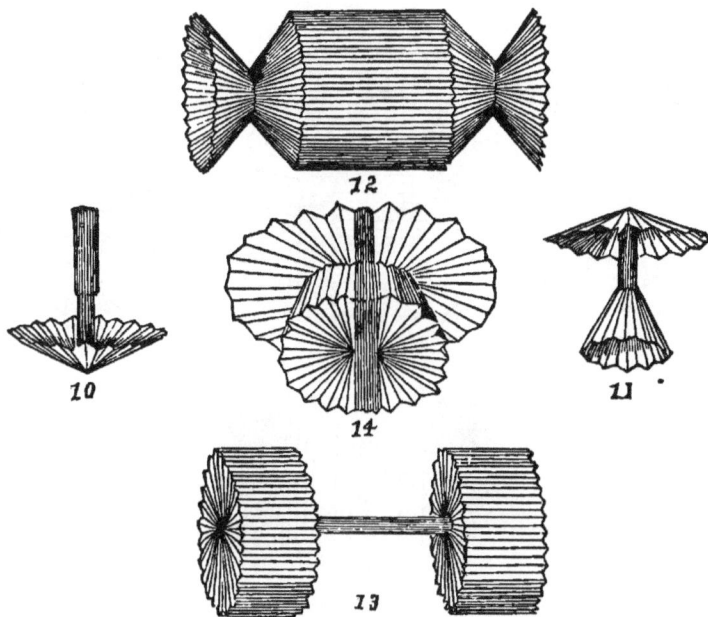

the central part, and by compressing the central folds well together, these wheels are produced (Fig. 13).

The hat, or cup and saucer (Fig. 14), is readily made by opening the paper out again, and catching it at the two ends.

We now come to a new form of subjects, so the original form (Fig. 5), must once more be reverted to. If the paper is caught at both ends, it can easily be folded so as

to form Fig. 15, and a table-mat may be made by drawing it out like Fig. 16.

A "nappie" dish, oval in form, and resembling Fig.
17, may be made from Fig. 16, by simply raising up the
sides *a* and *b*. By pressing the paper inward, Fig. 18 is

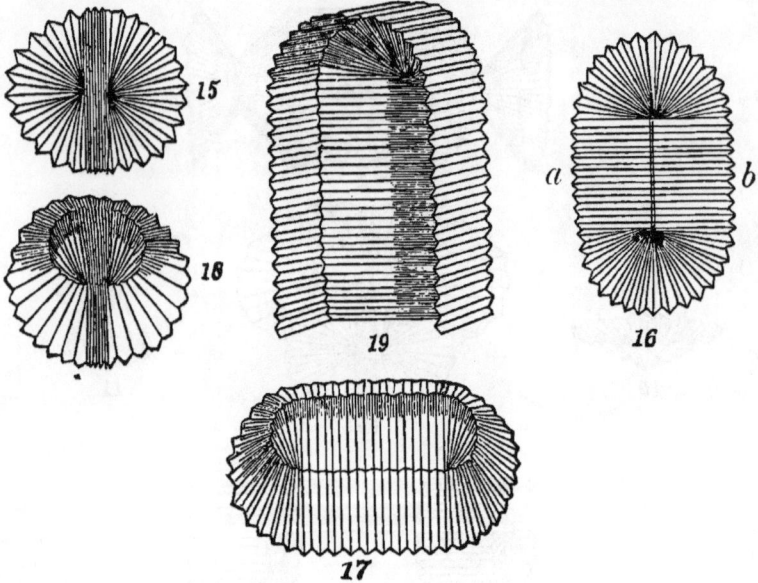

obtained. Fig. 19 is made by drawing the paper out
again, and letting it loose at the end. Thus you see, by
pulling out some parts and drawing in others, a quantity
of things could be made other than these I have shown.
It would be quite interesting if every boy and girl who
reads this, would try on some rainy day to see how near
to the sixty-five he or she could come. If two or three
friends in the same neighborhood should unite their

forces, and count all which are unlike, without reference to the maker, they might not fall so far short of the illustrious Japanese—I wish I could remember his name— after all.

THE MINIATURE YACHT AND HOW TO RIG HER.

Boat making and sailing are most fascinating pursuits, and we do not know but the old saying, "When a man has taken to boat-sailing, he is a sailor to the end of his days," is to a certain degree applicable to the boy who intelligently fits out his tiny craft, and sends her on little voyages across the neighboring pond.

If the sailing is to be done on water of any depth, there is one caution we should like to give at the very outset: *Learn to swim before you sail her.* No mere pleasure is worth risking one's life for, and accidents will happen even to the most careful boys.

After this, you may play on or near the water with as much safety as on the land.

Aside from the pleasure, one learns an extremely useful lesson in making a miniature model yacht, and in sailing her. A certain familiarity with the rigging, and the looks of the thing, will thus be obtained, and if your fingers have patiently set up shrouds and stays, and rove the mimic halyards, they will be less at sea with the ropes and stays of a real vessel.

Many boys living near the sea, and accustomed every day to see vessels lying at anchor, or sailing in and out of the harbor, have very hazy ideas concerning the rigging of any kind of craft. Well I remember in my early days of being obliged to run down to the wharf to see where to attach my topmast. Whether it belonged forward or aft of my mast I had not the slightest remembrance, and yet scarcely a day went by without my seeing a vessel in some form or other.

Boys are not the only persons, however, who look at things and do not see them. The power of minute and careful observation is a rare quality, and the majority of people go through life without forming the habit, or indeed dreaming they have not made the best use of their sight.

For the benefit of the boys who belong to this class, and those less fortunate ones living inland where yachts are unknown, I write this chapter.

In several of our large cities, ponds are set apart for the especial purpose of sailing toy vessels. They are the exclusive property of the boys, and any fine afternoon in season, and frequently out of season, if the ice does not interfere, crowds of boys may be seen sitting on the edges of these "lakes," intently watching the graceful fleet as it skims lightly over the water. The sixty-acre lake in Prospect Park, Brooklyn, and Conservatory Lake, Cen-

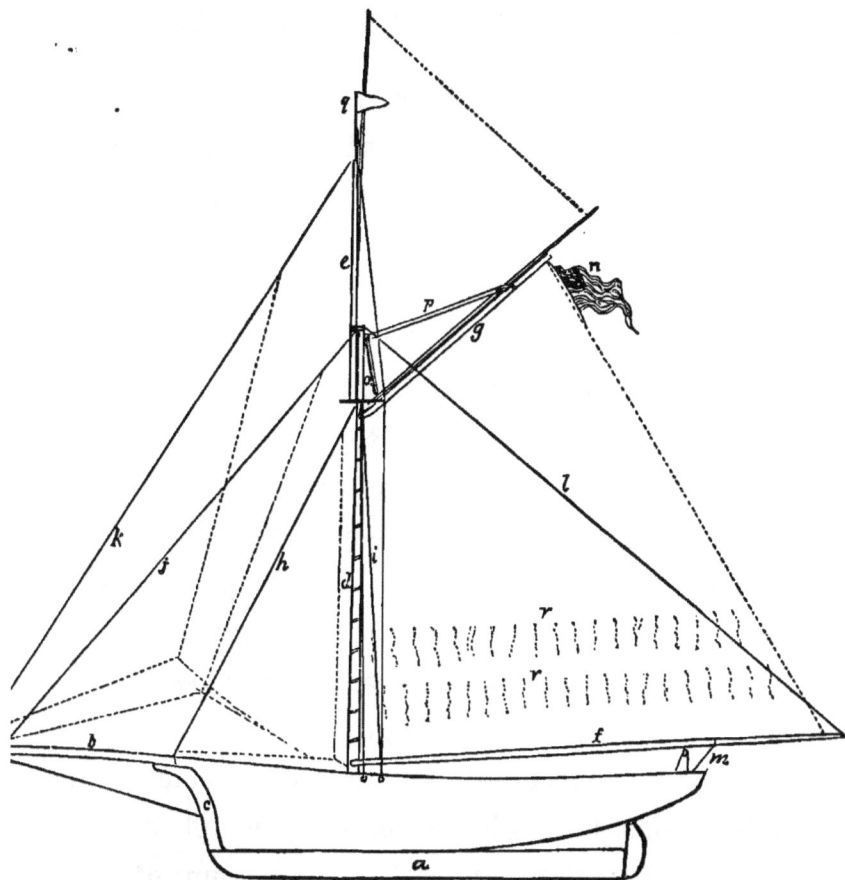

a Keel.	*j* Jib-stay.
b Bowsprit.	*k* Topmast-stay.
c Stern.	*l* Topping lift.
d Mast.	*m* Main-sheet.
e Topmast.	*n* Ensign.
f Boom.	*o* Throat halyards.
g Gaff.	*p* Peak halyards.
h Forestay.	*q* Burgee.
i Shrouds.	*r* Reef points.

tral Park, New York, are both set apart for the owners of these miniature yachts ; and it is wonderful how many older people, as well as the boys themselves, take interest in this amusement.

The building and sailing of tiny yachts is carried to a much greater extent in England than in this country. There the Prince of Wales is deeply interested in the sport, and has instituted a "Royal Yacht Club," presided over by himself, which has regular yacht regattas. These regattas take place on Serpentine Lake, in Hyde Park, every summer, and are considered quite important events. The yachts belonging to this club are very elegant affairs, one of them being valued at $5,000, yet none of them are over five feet in length.

We do not expect our boy readers to emulate their British cousins, but with the following simple directions we feel confident they can, with a fair amount of skill in the use of tools, and careful labor, make a very respectable miniature yacht, which shall be correct as far as she goes in both form and rigging.

In the fashioning of a miniature boat, the hull is the first thing which claims our attention ; and in making this, two elements are to be considered, rapidity and stability.

The rapidity or ease with which a vessel moves through water, is gained by a narrow hull—that is, narrow in proportion to its length—which, to be sure, renders the ves-

sel somewhat unstable ; but this instability may be overcome by loading the keel with lead. There is danger,
however, of carrying this to too great an extent, by low-
ering the vessel so much that the friction against her
sides more than counteracts the fine proportions of her
build. Hence a skillful designer reconciles these two
points.

There are two types of model recognized in yacht
building: First, the English cutter model, which is narrow, and quite deep in proportion to width, with its keel
heavily weighted to secure the necessary stability. This
model is best adapted to rough cruising in strong winds
and heavy seas, such as prevail on the English coasts.

Second, the American : This, our model, is much wider,
or, in nautical phrase, has much more beam in proportion
to length and depth. Indeed, it is often so shallow as to
merit the term "skimming-dish," ofttimes applied to this
class of vessels.

These boats are usually fitted with center-boards, which
can be lowered or raised according to the need of the
moment, instead of the deep keel of the English model,
American vessels having the advantage of smoother water
in which to make their cruises. The sheltered surface of
Long Island Sound and the bays which adjoin it at either
end, afford excellent sailing grounds for those owned in
New York and the vicinity.

For the toy boats our boys may desire to make, a medium between these two types will probably be found preferable in practice.

The center-board may be ruled out at once, as both itself and the well in which it plays would require more time and patience in their construction than most boys would care to give.

It is much better to have your boat too wide than too narrow, as a capsize is far more disconcerting to the average young yachtsman, than a slight inferiority of speed.

For a sloop yacht, the greatest width should be about one-third the length; and the point of greatest width, or beam, should be somewhat nearer the stern than bow.

Probably the best way to make a toy yacht is to procure a piece of wood, which is about three times as long as it is wide and deep, and whittle out your hull as your judgment or fancy may dictate; keeping in mind a few essential points, however, to insure ultimate success.

First, draw a line from the middle point of one end to the middle point of the other end of the top of the block; this will serve as a guide to the bow and the center of the stern. Care should be taken not to make your vessel too blunt at the bow; as a sailor would say, "the lines at the bow should be *fine* when they meet the water."

The elegant appearance of the boat is increased by giving an overhang to the stern, instead of running it up

vertically ; and if the young builder is confident in the
use of his tools, a sheer, as it is called, of the lines at the
top, or the gunwale, will add greatly to the grace of its
appearance.   For the benefit of those who do not understand the meaning of the word sheer, it may be explained
that it is the gradual and graceful downward curve from
bow to stern, noticeable in the bulwarks of vessels when
seen from one side.

It is perhaps superfluous to add that great care should
be taken to have each side of the craft alike, for if a pre-
ponderance of weight is on one side, the vessel will tip;
while if the curve is unequal, she will not sail evenly.

The hollowing out of the inside is most conveniently
accomplished with a sharp gouge and mallet, while the
hull is secured firmly in a vise.   When this is finished, a
hole should be made in the bottom to receive the lower
end of the mast, and care should be taken not to bore
through the hull, as it would be difficult to stop the in-
gress of water through it.

We have now come to the keel, which must be firmly
attached to the hull.   The best way to do this is to drive
three slender brass screws through the bottom of the boat,
with ends projecting from one-fourth to one-half an inch
along the line of the proposed keel.   Make a temporary
box around these, inclosing a space equal to the length
and breadth of the keel, with strips of thin wood, such as

cigar-box wood ; strips of heavy pasteboard may answer the purpose sufficiently well. In either case this mold should be firmly attached to the hull, in such a manner that after casting the keel it may be readily removed. Perhaps the best way to accomplish this is to paste it in place by means of narrow bands of stout paper. The inside of the mold must be rubbed with oil or lard to prevent the lead from adhering to its sides. This lead must be melted over a very hot fire, so that it will not cool too rapidly upon entering the mold, in which case it would not hold together as well. When cold, the mold may be detached, and the keel will be held firmly in place by the three screws.

The deck should be made of thin board, cut so as to accurately fit the top of your hull. If a sheer has been given to the bulwarks, it is of course much more difficult to fit the deck accurately, as it should follow the curve. It will very likely be found necessary to *steam* the board used, to make it sufficiently flexible. It will be possible to use stout pasteboard for the purpose, if both sides and edges are given a couple of coats of paint, which treatment should also be applied to the inside of the hole for the mast.

This hole should be placed very slightly farther astern than the hole already mentioned, made in the bottom of the vessel. The effect of this will be to give the mast a slight *rake*. This is always the case with the masts of a schooner yacht, but builders of sloop yachts occasionally omit the rake and "step" the mast in a vertical position.

The *bowsprit* may be fastened by two staples made of small wire, and driven down over it. One is driven down into the stem, or extreme forward point of the hull, and corresponds to what is called the "gammon iron" in a full-sized craft; the other secures the "inboard" end of the bowsprit, or that which is nearer the stern. This end is called the heel, and should nearly reach the mast. The outer end should project beyond the hull to a distance of nearly one-third the latter's length.

The rudder can be whittled from a thin piece of wood, in the shape shown in the figure; the upper part or head is round, and passes up through a hole in the overhang. The top of this rudder-head is squared off to fit the hole in the end of the tiller or helm. The rudder is "shipped" very much as a barn-door or window-blind is set in place. Suitable hinges for the rudder of a toy boat can be made of pins from which the heads have been filed. Two pins may be bent double for staples, and inserted into the "stern-post" of the vessel; while two others bent at right angles may be driven into the rudder, the projecting ends hanging down through the staples. The rudder should turn with sufficient friction to hold its place, at whatever angle it may be set. The hollow of the boat should not extend back into the overhang, as water might enter it through the rudder-hole.

The mast is composed of two parts or pieces ; the lower part is what is always understood when the "mast" is spoken of. The smaller piece, fastened to the upper end of the mast, is called the topmast.

The "mast," which extends above the deck to a distance equal to about three-fourths the length of the hull, passes through the hole in the deck already mentioned, and rests firmly in the hole made for it in the bottom of the hull.

The lower end of the topmast is lapped on in front of the upper end of the mast, as seen in the figure, and may be secured in place by two loops of fine brass wire.

The spars of next importance are those which stretch the mainsail. The larger is called the "boom," and extends along the lower edge or "foot" of the mainsail ; while the other, which is called the "gaff," is secured to its upper edge or "head." The boom is equal in length to the mast ; the usual meaning of the word is here intended, *i. e.*, the lower part. The gaff is a little over one-half the length of the boom.

The mast and topmast taper slightly toward their upper ends, while the gaff is nearly the same size throughout its entire length. The boom generally swells a little, being somewhat larger in the middle than at either end.

The boom and gaff are adjusted to the mast by a "jaw" on either side, forming a crotch, which keeps them from slipping off. Builders of miniature yachts will, however, probably find it more convenient to whittle the ends of the spars in the form of a crotch than to attach jaws as separate pieces.

Other smaller spars which enter into the equipment of racing craft, will be mentioned in speaking of the sails.

The *standing rigging* is now to be considered; this consists of stays and shrouds. "Shrouds" are ropes which lead from near the head of the mast to either side of the vessel, where they are fastened into the *chain-plates.* These are strong iron bands firmly bolted to the timbers. The shrouds of the model yacht, however, can be attached to copper tacks driven into the sides. They —the shrouds—are tied around the mast just below the point where the lower end of the topmast ends.

In "real" yachts these shrouds end in loops which encircle the mast, and rest upon, or are held in place by blocks called "hounds" attached to either side. But young ship-builders will probably find it will answer all purposes to make a slight notch on either side of the mast, at the point indicated.

A sloop yacht has usually two shrouds on either side,

while in a large ship there are four or five, making, as is known, a good-sized ladder.

The "fore-stay" runs from the same point on the mast to the top of stem.

In case the reader may be ignorant of the meaning of nautical terms, it may be well to say here that by "stem" is meant the piece of timber in the hull placed farthest forward, also called "forefoot" and "cutwater." The "fore-stay" may be passed through the staple already mentioned, which fastens the bowsprit to the hull. The jib-stay passes from mast-head to outer end of bowsprit.

The topmast-stay runs from the top of the topmast to the forward end of the bowsprit; here it is sometimes passed through a hole in the end, and brought down to the forefoot, near the water line.

The bob-stay runs from the end of the bowsprit to the stem, and acts as a brace to offset the strain of the "headsails," or the sails in front of the mast. In a large yacht it is necessary that this stay be very strong; and in such cases it is often a substantial strip of iron or steel.

A yacht has, also, what are called "backstays," which run on either side from head of "topmast" to points on the sides somewhat abaft, or back of the places where the shrouds are attached.

There are also "cross-trees," with "topmast shrouds"

leading from them to the top of the topmast; but these, as well as the backstays, may as well be dispensed with by our juvenile naval architect, as a complication of unnecessary cords is to be avoided on a miniature craft.

We must now take up the sails, the most important of which is the mainsail. The shape of this may be sufficiently well understood from the figure. The edge next the mast is called the "luff," while the outer or longer side opposite to this is called the "leech." The upper and lower edges are called respectively the "head" and "foot." The lower after corner of this sail is called the "clew," the lower fore corner the "tack," while the upper after corner is called the "peak."

The "mast-hoops" are attached to the "luff" and run up and down the mast as the sail is raised or lowered. In vessels of miniature size, these may be supplied by small brass curtain rings. The "foresail" also runs on small rings or loops which slide on the forestay. The jib, in like manner, is attached to the "jib-stay"; the "jib-top-sail" or "flying-jib" to topmast-stay.

It may be well to dispense with the forestay, and to enlarge the jib so as to occupy the additional space thus given, as the work will be less, and the appearance quite as good.

It now remains to consider the "gaff-topsail," which occupies the space between the topmast and the gaff.

This sail is set in quite a number of ways; in a sloop yacht it is usual to stretch it on two light spars, which are contiguous to mast and gaff.

Beside these, racing yachts in light winds carry a "balloon jib," which is simply an extremely large jib-topsail; and a "spinnaker," which is used in going before the wind. It is shaped like a large jib, and is spread by means of a small spar extending along its foot, called the "spinnaker boom," so that it may take the wind on the side opposite the mainsail.

These sails are spread by means of *running* rigging. First, the *halyards*, by means of which the sails are hoisted. The mainsail usually has two halyards, one line being attached to the gaff near where it touches the mast, which is called the "throat halyards." The other is smaller, encountering less strain, and is termed "peak halyards," as it raises that part of the sail after the luff has been hoisted.

The gaff-topsail of a regular yacht also has two halyards, one of which raises the edge next the mast, and the other draws its foot out to end of gaff.

The "jibs" are each raised by one "halyard" attached to head or upper corner.

In a small boat like that we are considering, one halyard for each sail will be amply sufficient. In fact it is a frequent practice to keep the sails permanently spread;

which has this in its favor, that they are much smoother, much less wrinkled, than when furled between cruises.

The "topping lift" is a line which leads from the head of the "mast" to the outer end of the "boom," which it keeps from falling on deck when sail is lowered.

The *sheets* are not sails, as the reader not conversant with nautical expressions would suppose, but ropes, or lines, which keep the sails in their proper position in respect to the wind. The *main-sheet*, which controls the mainsail, is attached to the boom at a point just above the stern, to which the other end is led. Here it is fastened to a cleat.

The sheets of the headsails are fastened to their "clews" or lower aft corners, and led to cleats near foot of mast. In large craft the sheets are passed through a number of pulleys in order to secure sufficient purchase.

In addition to the rigging already mentioned, many other ropes might be enumerated, such as the "down-hauls," "outhauls," "spinnaker brace and guy," "bow-sprit shrouds," etc., but as has already been said, the less confusion of cords in a miniature craft, the better.

A SCHOONER YACHT.

In this the length should be greater in proportion to its other dimensions than in the sloop yacht. The mainmast should be stepped a little abaft the middle point of the hull. The foremast is stepped about midway between the mainmast and the stem, and should be very nearly as high as the mainmast. The foretop-mast, however, should be decidedly shorter than the maintop-mast.

The bowsprit of the schooner yacht should be somewhat thicker and shorter in proportion than that of the sloop yacht, and is lengthened to the desired extent by means of a small spar resting on its top, which is called the jib-boom.

The forestay comes down to the bowsprit head, instead of to the stem. The jib-stay runs from the mast-head to the jib-boom, through which it passes a short distance from the end of the latter. The topmast stay extends from the upper part of the topmast to the end of the jib-boom. The two latter stays pass from the jib-boom to the "martingale," a short spar, which has a hook at its upper end. This hook passes through an iron ring on the under side of the head of the bowsprit.

The martingale extends downward toward the water, while the stays pass through it, or through iron loops affixed to either side, and are fastened to the stem or the upper part of the bows.

As in the sloop, one or more stout bobstays connect the bowsprit head with the stem.

The two masts are braced together by means of certain

stays, of which the most important is the *spring-stay*, which connects the mast-heads. Two other stays extend from the maintop-mast to the foremast head. (See figure.)

| *a* Mainmast. | *c* Bowsprit. | *e* Martingale. |
| *b* Foremast. | *d* Jib-boom. | *f* Spring-stay. |

The mainsail and its gaff-topsail are similar to those of the sloop, but the foresail is much smaller, as it must pass between the masts in tacking, and varies little in breadth from head to foot.

A schooner yacht has a maintop-mast staysail, which is used in racing, and comes down nearly to the deck. Its sheet is rove through a block at the after end of the boom, whence it is brought back to the stern and "belayed" to a cleat.

"Belaying" is the nautical term for winding a rope on a cleat or belaying pin ; which is done as a boy winds his kite string, on each end alternately, in figure-eight style.

The fore gaff-topsail is not provided with spars or booms at its edges, but has rings along its luff, like those of the lower sails, which run on the foretop-mast.

The sails of a large vessel have ropes called bolt-ropes, sewed entirely around their edges, which may, of course, be dispensed with in the sails of the miniature yacht, as they will be sufficiently strong without such aid.

The reef-points are short lengths of small rope, arranged at equal distances from each other, in rows parallel to the booms ; they pass through the sail and hang down on either side. There are usually two rows of these on the foresail, and three on the mainsail, while the larger headsails are also provided with them.

Before the sails are put on or *bent,* it will be advisable to paint the yacht. A coat of paint should have been given to the inside of hull as well as under side of deck, to prevent the wood from becoming water-soaked in case of leakage.

Custom has rigidly prescribed the colors for the exterior of a yacht, above the water line ; either black or white, with a narrow gold line below the gunwale, being universally employed. Below the water line greater latitude may be given to individual taste; either dark green, brown, or black, may be used, according to the preference of the owner.

The greatest pains are taken to keep the bottom of a racing yacht in the smoothest possible condition. It is usually covered with black-lead and polished to the utmost degree. This treatment is often renewed three or four times in the course of a season.

The mast should not be painted, but stained a bright yellow, with a little raw sienna in oil. When dry it should be shellacked; in fact, the latter will form a good coating for the painted surface of the hull as well. If the shellac be thick, it may of itself stain the mast to a sufficient extent, but in that case—if thick—it should not be used on the white hull. The short space where the mainmast and topmast overlap each other should be painted the color of the hull. The bowsprit should be the color of the hull, and the jib-boom stained like the masts. The deck may be painted with white, to which enough sienna has been added to give it a buff tint.

The prow, or upper portion of stem just below the bowsprit, is usually carved and gilded; and the stem is occasionally decorated in like manner; but although there seems to be no limit to the increasing richness and elegance of the interior of our American yachts, the tendency of the time leads more and more toward a severely plain and quiet treatment of the exterior.

A yacht always carries a little triangular flag at the topmast-head called the "burgee."

A schooner yacht, of course, flies two of them, one at each mast-head. These are simultaneously hauled down at the moment of sunset. A national flag, called the "ensign," is generally hoisted at the peak of the mainsail.

These instructions apply equally well to the papier-maché boats described at page 90, which have the advantages of lightness and ease of construction.

www.ingramcontent.com/pod-product-compliance
Lightning Source LLC
Chambersburg PA
CBHW021111270326
41929CB00009B/831